The End
of the Dream

John G. Neihardt

The End of the Dream

& Other Stories

Compiled by
Hilda Neihardt Petri
with an introduction
by Jay Fultz

University of Nebraska Press
Lincoln and London

Copyright © 1991 by the
University of Nebraska Press
All rights reserved
Manufactured in the United
States of America
The paper in this book meets
the minimum requirements
of American National
Standard for Information
Sciences – Permanence
of Paper for
Printed Library Materials,
ANSI Z39.48 – 1984.
Library of Congress Cataloging-
in-Publication Data
Neihardt, John Gneisenau,
1881–1973.
The end of the dream and
other stories by
John G. Neihardt ;
compiled by Hilda Neihardt
Petri ; with an introduction
by Jay Fultz.
p. cm. Includes biblio-
graphical references.
ISBN 0-8032-3326-4 (cl : alk)
1. Omaha Indians – Fiction.
2. Indians of North America –
Nebraska – Fiction.
I. Petri, Hilda Neihardt.
II. Title. PS3527.E35A6 1991
813'.52 – dc20   90-43667 CIP

"I slept and awoke, and lo!
the sun was teaching gladness to the hills."

—"The End of the Dream"

I am indebted to the late
Professor Lucile F. Aly,
whose interest in my father's
early short stories
led her to begin collecting them
when this book was still a dream.

HILDA NEIHARDT PETRI

Contents

Introduction

By Jay Fultz

Natty Bumppo's noble companion Chingachgook, the fiendish Black Vulture of *Nick of the Woods,* the mournful Hiawatha and romantic Pocahontas, the Injun Joe of Tom Sawyer's nightmares—all these literary shades gathered round as John G. Neihardt reviewed a book for the *St. Louis Post-Dispatch* one day in 1927. "From Cooper onward it is true that the Indian has been misrepresented," he wrote. "Either he was a painted white man with feathers, as in Cooper, or a bloodthirsty brute, as in the lurid thrillers, or a milksop, as in Longfellow, or an interesting subject for dilletant enthusiasms. The only way to understand a race is to get inside the racial consciousness through intimate and sympathetic contact."[1]

At the beginning of his career Neihardt had written short stories of sufficient Indian cast to perplex the critics. About two-thirds of the more than thirty stories he produced from 1901 to 1908, when he was in his twenties, were inspired by his association with the Omahas at their reservation near his home in Bancroft, Nebraska. As clerk to a trader, he collected debts from Indians who had been defrauded of their lands by fast-talking bargain hunters. Deeply moved by the plight of the displaced "long hairs," Neihardt won their trust and affection. "I have sat in their lodges and tepees, eaten their meat, drunk their soup, smoked their pipes, and coddled their babies," he told a friend. Three decades before he wrote the work that would link him eternally with Black Elk's people, Neihardt was like a brother to the Omahas, who named him Little Bull Buffalo. Although shaped by his imagination, the short stories that came out of his experience at the reservation turned away from literary tradition to present not showcase Indians but human beings "in the grip of fate."[2]

The nine stories in this collection were published from 1901 to 1905 in the *Overland Monthly,* an illustrated magazine that since 1868 had interpreted the West, particularly California, for sophisticated easterners. First edited by Bret Harte, whose "Outcasts of Poker Flat" appeared in the second number, the magazine paraded the talents of Mark Twain and Jack London, the fiction of now-forgotten writers like May E. Southworth and Agnes Lockhart Hughes, and articles on everything from theosophy to gold hunting on Queen Charlotte's Island. Indians were a favorite topic, and the general run of stories about them now compare to Neihardt's as passable (and sometimes tarnished) plateware does to good silver. For example, the jaw-breaking biblical language of Cromwell Galpin's "The Corn People: A Story of Zuni" is a far cry from the natural eloquence of Neihardt's "The Singing of the Frogs," which also appeared in the September 1901 issue of the *Overland Monthly.* In the following years the magazine published more stories by Neihardt that granted the Indians their full humanity, but still more by writers who portrayed them as "shiftless" and "treacherous," as heathens to be converted by Christian missionaries, as sentimental projections of white guilt, or as cardboard figures in melodrama. Perhaps the ultimate in patronization, unconscious and otherwise, can be seen in a 1906 story about a servant named Indian Kate, who was "thoroughly clean about her work and person," although "the mark of her tribe on her chin was most disfiguring." A slow-moving domestic ("Indians were never known to be swift"), she muffs her chance for improvement by returning to her tribe. "Once an Indian, always an Indian," the narrator concludes.[3]

Viewed in the context of the literary culture of their time, Neihardt's Indian stories stand up very respectably, and a closer look should reveal why Dr. Susan LaFlesche Picotte, the daughter of Joseph LaFlesche (Iron Eyes), last chief of the Omahas, praised them for their "true understanding of Indian character." Indeed, Neihardt's Indians were the only ones in literature from Cooper to Frederic Remington that had not offended her![4] The uniqueness of the stories collected here is due, in part, to their revelation of Omaha culture. It is hard to say how much Neihardt had learned from books. Although some writings on the Omahas were available,[5] the tribe had no written record. Alice Fletcher and Francis LaFlesche would not publish their definitive *Omaha Tribe* until 1911; yet in the early "When the Snows Drift" Neihardt describes the layout of a winter village essentially as they would. That story, as well as "The Singing of the Frogs," is true to history in presenting the seven chiefs of the council, who smoke their long red pipes while deliberating on matters of moment. In all of the stories various rituals and ceremonies are noted with an easy familiarity unexpected in a white writer just getting started. Three of them—"The Triumph of Seha," "The Smile of God," and "The End of the Dream"—are patterned on a young man's vision quest, with an ethnologist's attention to detail. The number four, emphasized in several of the stories and implying the four sacred directions, is just one sign of the mysticism that surrounded an Indian from birth to death.[6] Susan LaFlesche Picotte thought Neihardt was in sympathy with that essential aspect of her people's character to an unprecedented degree.

When "The End of the Dream" and other stories were collected in *The Lonesome Trail* in 1907, Dr. Picotte wrote, in a letter to the *New York Times,* that Neihardt's Indians were "flesh and blood, with the same cardinal virtues and the same cardinal sins . . . as the rest of humankind."[7] Love and hate, kindness and cruelty, hope and despair, generosity and envy, honesty and guile, spiritual impulse and sexual desire operate in the wholly Indian world of these stories. All but one, "A Prairie Borgia," are set in the time before contact with white men. This occurred before the end of the seventeenth century, when the Omahas traded with Frenchmen who had established posts west of the Great Lakes. Removed from the French and Indian War, they never fought against the white race and remained relatively isolated until the last decade of the eighteenth century, when white fur traders visited them in present-day eastern Nebraska.[8] In "A Prairie Borgia," the despotic chief Wazhinga Saba (clearly Blackbird) obtains whiskey and finally poison from the white traders to carry out his machinations against a rival. Cursed by the dying victim, he succumbs (as Chief Blackbird did) to the disease (smallpox) that had wiped out two-thirds of the Omahas by the time Lewis and Clark encountered their village in 1804.

The power-hungry Wazhinga Saba (Neihardt notes that he was buried with his weapons on Blackbird Hill, sitting upon his horse so that he might see the white men round the river in their canoes)[9] is the worst of the medicine men because he subjugates his people through magic and trickery. In "The Smile of God," the medicine man Ashunhunga cannot end the famine afflicting his tribe. In desperation, he unjustly fingers a cripple as the "black spirit" causing it. In "The End of the Dream," the medicine man's "most potent songs" and "most mysterious rites" fail to stop the spread of a plague. And in "The Triumph of Seha," a personable and popular youth, destined to become a seer, must face down a jealous medicine man. The portrayal of the medicine man in the early stories may owe something to the nineteenth-century literary tradition that usually presented him as crafty and manipulative.[10] It should be remembered that these are imaginative constructions, reworkings and intensifications of the Omahas' tales of the old days. Their "Indian-

ness" is not diluted by the dramatic imperative of con-
flict—here, a struggle for power.

The powerless who win some sort of victory are
nearly always social outcasts. The misshapen and despised cripple in "The Smile of God," the unwarriorlike
son who is scorned as unmanly in "The End of the
Dream"—both set out on lonely quests to save their
people from catastrophe and to gain acceptance. Both are
directed by the power of absolute, single-minded belief.
In aspiring hugely both tempt fate. And both inspire in
the villagers they long to join the kind of uncompre-
hending wonder that leads to legend. Another outcast,
Little Wolf, who in "The Beating of the War Drums" is
taunted because his size disqualifies him for warrior-
hood, also tries singlehandedly to prove his worth. But
his ruse to save the women captured by the Otoes, in-
cluding the girl of his dreams, has an unexpected out-
come because he cannot escape the wolflike self-image
that has been formed by years of cruel teasing. Loss
brings a gain of the sort beyond dreams. Similarly, in
"When the Snow Drifts," the murderer who has been
exiled inspires the pity of a woman whose devotion joins
her fate to his. (Indeed, romantic love is nearly always
doomed.)

What is to be made of the central role assigned to the
misfit in these stories and in those collected in *Indian Tales
and Others* (1927)? Lucile F. Aly suggests that in one incar-
nation he or she is the artist in an unappreciative world,[11]
and certainly the characterizing imagery often conveys a
sensibility not shared by coarser types, a rare capacity for

suffering and joy, a communion with the universe. Lawrence J. Evers has discussed a basic pattern of the Omaha myths: the protagonist initially stands outside his society and is integrated into it either by becoming a husband or father or by assuming the role of protector and provider through warfare and hunting. The pattern is seen in "a series of moves from disequilibrium to equilibrium."[12] It may be applied to these stories, but there is a double dimension: the character who is at odds with society is at the same time at one with nature, or is inclined to be so through simple-minded innocence or through reflection imposed by solitude (an exception is the murderer, who commits an act against nature). The *society* that is at odds with the natural order—a situation symbolized by drought, famine, epidemics—needs the intercession of one who is not, but at the same time it still does not assimilate the one who restores equilibrium or stability since his or her heroism is essentially unfathomable, to be distanced by myth if recognized at all. In those stories in which the outcast yearns for love (the murderer in "When the Snow Drift," the reclusive title character of "The Fading of Shadow Flower," Little Wolf in "The Beating of the War Drums," the woman in "The Singing of the Frogs" who is rejected by a warrior obsessed with his horse, the cast-off children who play at being married in "The End of the Dream") fulfillment is likely to take a form as abstract and elusive as that realized by those lovers on Keats's Grecian urn.

Insatiable and sometimes unrequited love, sacrifice, the tooth-and-tomahawk war for power, revenge, the

quest for spiritual attainment—these themes weave in
and out of the stories in this collection. They have often
been dismissed as apprentice work by scholars, but they
are distinguished by an inwardness that is reflected in the
elaborate imagery. Neihardt's philosophical affinity for
the Omaha view of all life as closely interrelated is better
known than his understanding of psychology. Ghastly
concrete demons pursue a conscience-stricken murderer.
The suggestible Little Wolf becomes, in his own mind,
what his tormentors call him—that animal the Indians associated with humankind's restless destructiveness. The
rite of *Wazhinadee* was directed against a tribesman who
had offended social order and endangered his people. In
"The Triumph of Seha" the envious medicine man, wish-
ing to turn public opinion against the hero, persuades the
elders to direct their thoughts against him. Thus Seha
must reckon with a force as inexorable as any tangible
one. According to Fletcher and LaFlesche, "This form of
punishment, which blended social ostracism with a kind
of magical power, was greatly feared and frequently
resulted in the death of the victim."[13]

Other stories have a profound psychological dimension. Shadow Flower describes her depression in terms
of nature ("the prairie is so cold and white, so cold and
white"), and her descending madness takes her into the
moonlit mist in search of summer. Neihardt does not
say, in "The Smile of God," what the silent women
tending the fire are thinking or feeling, but the image of
the fire whose "ruddy tongues" send "their voices roaring up the hills" to be echoed by the faint "lowing of a

phantom herd" suggests metaphorically their hungry, desperate preoccupation with finding the buffalo.

When these stories were first published, some reviewers complained that their language was excessively rhetorical. "Neihardt gives us an over-accumulation of vivid detail which defeats its own ends," wrote the critic for the *Saturday Review*.[14] But a close reading reveals his artistry in using chains of imagery that delineate inner and outer states at once. Throughout *The End of the Dream and Other Stories* the repetition and subtle variation of imagery advances character and narrative movement while it pictures the setting and creates atmosphere. If the imagery is not as close-knit in Neihardt's stories as it is in Henry James's novels, it nevertheless helps to structure them. For example, in "When the Snows Drift" Mun-chpe thinks that he deserves to receive the eagle feather because he killed a Sioux chief during a battle in which he fought "so closely that he breathed the breath of his foe." That arresting image is repeated in his plea for the honor before the chiefs of counsel. After killing the rival wearing *his* feather, Mun-chpe is pursued by the dead man's frightful spirit, which presses "its blue lips against [his] lips" and seems to be "drinking his breath." During his winter of exile he summons in a dream the woman for whom he wished to win the feather. She finds him during a wailing storm, and presses her lips against his in a quietly horrifying fade-out. The image of the fatal kiss appears in four stages of the story, changing with the dramatic context.

This metaphorical language flows in complex rhythms,

seeming to catch an Indian idiom.[15] The classical allu-
sions that would permeate *A Cycle of the West* are held to a
minimum in these stories with mention of Leander and
the Hellespont and "a bronze Colossus." The word *red-
skin,* which had peppered so many dime novels, never
once appears here; and although *squaw* and *papoose* do,
they were part of the literary currency and popular usage
of that era. Anyhow, Neihardt's deep feeling for his
material does not permit a patronizing tone.

The best of the stories are like tapestries in which
images coalesce into a general design. In his book reviews, Neihardt decried the formlessness and fragmen-
tation of much contemporary writing. As late as 1967 he
expressed disgust for twentieth-century literature that
was prone to exhibit life as "one damned thing after another, patternless and futile." The stories collected here
are more tightly organized than they would first appear
to be. Lucile Aly is right in saying that they show Neihardt "exploring techniques, experimenting with structures, and developing his style."[16] The frame format is
not as conspicuous in this collection as it is in *Indian Tales
and Others,* but a good example of it is "The Spirit of
Crow Butte," in which the narrator recalls a legend
about a Crow warrior who sacrificed his life to save his
companions; a variation of it is included in George Bird
Grinnell's *Pawnee Hero Stories and Folk-Tales.*[17] There is a
progression in Neihardt's mastery of form from "When
the Snows Drift" (1901) to "The End of the Dream"
(1905). The latter, in particular, is well made.

"The End of the Dream" is being told after the death

of Gunthai, whose son was like the sun to her. As she weaves baskets she tries to interest him in becoming a warrior like his late father but is disappointed to see no response. Time passes and when the son, Nu Zhinga, develops "the visible body of a black spirit's joke" he is jeered by the villagers. He lives in his own little world, inhabited by Gunthai, a tame gray wolf, and Tabea, his crippled playmate. At puberty Nu Zhinga goes to the "high hill of dreams" to summon a vision. In doing so he fails to meet expectations. That fall Nu Zhinga is tested again when he rides out with a war party, but his conduct in battle brings grief to Gunthai. In the winter a plague spreads through the village, resisting not only the attempts of the women to bar the "black spirit" by covering doors but also the rites of the medicine man, who dreams that a tuft of hair from the white bison will save his people.[18] The same dream occurs to Nu Zhinga, who in the morning goes out with his tame wolf to find the tuft and redeem himself. Meanwhile, the people panic and trample over each other in fleeing the village. Several evenings later a lone figure accompanied by a wolf comes to the hill overlooking the village. He waves a tuft of hair from the albino bison and shouts that "the black spirits" have been routed. His face is wolflike; the wolf's eyes are half-human. On discovering desolation, he falls down in the snow. Days pass and the homesick villagers come back to die, only to find that the disease has fled. Who has saved them from "the black spirits"? The answer is the supreme irony on which this story turns.

The elaborate design of "The End of the Dream" may

be evident even from the summary above. Various lines of imagery draw it into the tightest unity, often with ironic effect. Gunthai's weaving links her with one of the Fates of classical mythology; she spins a warrior's future for him. Weaving is associated with time: "the days of sun and snow wove themselves into years." Her weaving stops momentarily when he goes on his vision quest. Most pervasive is the nature imagery. Nu Zhinga is a child of the cosmos: his starlike eyes have a spiritual luminosity and he and the other outcast, Tabea, are connected with the sunshine. The stars glow kindly, like his own eyes, during the vision quest. His capacity for hope and joy never deserts him. In contrast, the ambitious Gunthai is shown to be at cross-purposes with the universe: "there was night for her in the brightest noon." Similarly, the mysterious disease that rages through the village is symptomatic of something wrong in the human relation to the natural order: while the weather freezes, the fever in the blood blazes. The flight of the villagers who act selfishly to save their own skins symbolizes the breakdown of that communal spirit so vital to continued life. Nu Zhinga's unbidden dream of the sacred white buffalo is his long-delayed vision. Interestingly, the imagery surrounding Nu Zhinga when he has accomplished his mission suggests, in Blakean terms, that he has passed from innocence into experience. To some extent, he and the tame wolf exchange identities; and it is the wolf, howling like the wind, that is last heard. (In childhood Nu Zhinga had sung like the wind to Tabea.) The "black spirits" imagery culminates in a double irony because the villagers do not understand what they say.

The story is structured not only through the imagery but through parallel scenes or movements. Nu Zhinga goes four times to the "hill of dreams" to seek a vision; his hopeful mother watches from the village the first time. The situation is reversed when he leaves the village for war: his mother and Tabea watch from the hill with renewed hope. Nu Zhinga stands on the hill again when he returns from hunting the white bison, and then he goes down into the valley of death (as the imagery makes clear). In the scene immediately following, the advance scout and the surviving villagers stand on the hill and then go down to the village and renewed life. But this line of imagery has not been exhausted: Nu Zhinga and Tabea in childhood are associated with "the summer hills," while the warriors tramp across shivering "brown hills" and the first victim of the plague is buried on a hill in wintertime. There are other arresting parallelisms. When Nu Zhinga goes to war, his mother arms him with his father's bow and arrows, but he is a reluctant warrior and hardly deserves to join in the "song of victory." After the dream-vision of the sacred buffalo comes to him, he arms himself with his father's bow and arrows and walks to his great solitary engagement, his excitement reaching the "fury of a battle-song."

This may be enough to suggest how carefully Neihardt ordered language and designed scenes to achieve a satisfying and meaningful artistic unity. The author of "The End of the Dream" and other stories in this collection was a master wordman and a conscious craftsman. Yet there were few critics of an expansive Whitmanesque spirit to welcome him at the threshold of a brilliant career. Reviewers of *The Lonesome Trail,* containing five of the stories collected here, tempered their praise. One thought that "despite their undeniable charm and vivid manner" in picturing the life of the Indian, they left "a distinctly depressing effect on the mind." Another ventured that some of the stories were "excellent specimens of their class" but predicted the author would "do better work when he [had] learnt restraint."[19] That work has been in for some time now and it is possible to see that John G. Neihardt, steeped in the rhythms and motifs and structures of oral native literature, was from the beginning a disciplined creative artist.

NOTES

I am indebted to Hilda Neihardt Petri, who compiled these stories and made the reprinting of them possible, for her information and interest; and to Raymond J. DeMallie, professor of anthropology and director of the American Indian Studies Research Institute at Indiana University, and Paul A. Olson, an authority on the Omaha Indians and Foundation Professor of English at the University of Nebraska–Lincoln, for their generous help in reading a draft of the introduction and offering advice.

1. Review of *The American Indian, North, South, and Central,* by Hyatt Verrill, *St. Louis Post-Dispatch,* March 28, 1927, p. 15.

2. Letter to Bob Davis, November 14, 1905, Davis Col-

lection, Manuscripts Division, New York City Public Library; letter to Julius T. House, August 25, 1929, collection in the possession of Mary House Ryskind; both quoted in Lucile F. Aly, *John G. Neihardt: A Critical Biography* (Amsterdam: Rodopi, 1977), pp. 33–34.

3. Helen A. Martin, "Indian Kate," *Overland Monthly* 47 (June 1906): 29–30. To be sure, some white writers were sympathetic to the Indian. Hamlin Garland, for example, was writing his Indian stories (finally collected in 1923 in *The Book of the American Indian*) at the same time as Neihardt. Roy W. Meyer thinks that although Garland sometimes achieved "fair success" in attempting to write from the Indian's point of view, he was "never entirely convincing" in doing so. See "Hamlin Garland and the American Indian," *Western American Literature* 2 (1967): 121.

4. John G. Neihardt, *Patterns and Coincidences: A Sequel to "All Is But a Beginning"* (Columbia: University of Missouri Press, 1978), p. 40.

5. Rev. J. Owen Dorsey's *Omaha Sociology* was originally published as an annual report of the U.S. Bureau of Ethnology in 1884. Neihardt may have been familiar with the writings of explorers, in particular Edwin James's account of Stephen H. Long's expedition of 1820, which describes the Omahas. To speculate further, he could have read Alice Fletcher's articles about the tribe in *Century Magazine* late in the nineteenth century. See, for example, "Tribal Life among the Omahas," which appeared in vol. 51 (January 1896): 450–61.

6. Alice C. Fletcher and Francis LaFlesche, *The Omaha Tribe,* Twenty-Seventh Annual Report of the Bureau of American Ethnology to the Secretary of the Smithsonian Institution, 1905–1906 (1911; reprint, 2 vols., Lincoln: University of Nebraska Press, 1972), 1:134–98, 206–16, 128–33. See also Paul A. Olson, ed., *The Book of the Omaha:*

Literature of the Omaha People (Lincoln: Nebraska Curriculum Development Center, 1979).

7. Letter to the *New York Times,* June 15, 1907.

8. Fletcher and LaFlesche, *The Omaha Tribe,* 2:611–13.

9. The story of Blackbird's burial appears in George Catlin, *Manners, Customs and Condition of the North American Indians,* 2 vols. (London: Henry G. Bohn, 1857), 2:5–6.

10. George Elwood Jones, Jr., "The American Indian in the American Novel, 1875–1950" (Ph.D. diss., New York University, 1958), pp. 230–37. By the time Neihardt wrote his stories the authority of the traditional medicine man was being eroded by the influence of Christian missionaries and the peyote religion.

11. Lucile F. Aly, "Trappers and Indians," in *A Sender of Words: Essays in Memory of John G. Neihardt,* ed. Vine Deloria, Jr. (Salt Lake City: Howe Brothers, 1984), p. 76. Compare Neihardt's outcasts with the traditional figure of the orphan in Omaha stories. See, for example, "Orphan and the Monkey" in Olson, *The Book of the Omaha,* pp. 92–101.

12. Lawrence J. Evers, "The Literature of the Omaha" (Ph.D. diss., University of Nebraska–Lincoln, 1972), p. 56.

13. Fletcher and LaFlesche, *The Omaha Tribe,* 1:71; 2: 583–84.

14. Review of John G. Neihardt's *The Lonesome Trail, Saturday Review* 104 (September 21, 1907): 369.

15. The point is made by Aly in "Trappers and Indians," p. 73.

16. John G. Neihardt, interview by John Thomas Richards, Skyrim Farm, July 26, 1967, quoted in Richards, *Luminous Sanity: Literary Criticism Written by John G. Neihardt* (Cape Girardeau, Mo.: Concord Publishing House, 1973), p. 140; Aly, "Trappers and Indians," p. 72.

17. Compare "The Prisoners of Court House Rock" in George Bird Grinnell, *Pawnee Hero Stories and Folk-Tales* (1889; reprint, Lincoln: University of Nebraska Press, 1961), pp. 67–69.

18. For a discussion of the significance of the white buffalo hide in Omaha culture, see Fletcher and LaFlesche, *The Omaha Tribe,* 1:283–87.

19. "The Fading of Shadow Flower," "The Triumph of Seha," "The End of the Dream," "The Beating of the War Drums," and "The Smile of God" were included in *The Lonesome Trail.* The reviews quoted here appeared in *Arena* 38 (August 1907): 222, and *Academy* (London) 72 (June 22, 1907): 610.

The End of
the Dream

When the Snows Drift

All through the "month of the bellowing of the bulls" the war with the Sioux had raged: all through the dry hot "month of the sunflowers" the sound of the hurrying battle had swept the broad brown plains like the angry voice of a prairie fire, when the Southwest booms. But now the fight was ended; the beaten Sioux had carried their wrath and defeat with them into the North; and the Pawnees, allies of the Omahas, had taken their way into the South, to build their village in the wooded bottoms of the broad and shallow stream.

On the banks of a creek the Omahas had built their winter village. The tepees were constructed by driving trimmed willow boughs into the ground in the shape of a cone, about which buffalo hides and bark were securely fastened, leaving an opening at the top, through which the smoke of the winter fire might pass.

In accordance with an ancient custom, the village was built in a great circle with an opening to the east. One standing in this opening and facing the west would divide the tribe with his line of vision into two bands, the one to his right would be the Hunga Band, the duty of

I

which is to defend the holy relics. The one to his left would be the Ishta Sunda band, or the "thunder men." To the right, within the circle and near the opening, would stand the lodge of the council, consisting of seven chiefs, and the great tepee where the totem pole and the holy relics are kept. This has ever been the village of the Omaha.

The tribe was happy; for its inveterate enemy, the Sioux, had been driven with broken bows against the blowing of the north wind.

The tribe was glad; but none so glad as Mun-chpe (Cloud.) As he sat in his tepee with the thunder men, he was thinking of how proudly he would ride his pony before the old chiefs, when the pow-wow was held over the recent victory. Yes, he would ride swiftly past the smoking council, and they would call him to them and place the eagle feather in his hair, for had he not touched and slain a big Sioux chief, fighting so closely that he breathed the breath of his foe? "Hi–Hi!" his heart cried within him as he thought. Would not the whole tribe shout? Would not the old men say "Mun-chpe is a brave youth?" Perhaps the big medicine man, Wa-zhing-a Sa-ba (Blackbird) himself, would praise him, as he dashed around the circle on his fleet pony, with the shout on his lips and the eagle feather in his hair! Yes, and *she* would see him: Wa-te-na would see him, and then she would be proud to be his squaw. "Hi hi!" he shouted with his great gladness; for he was a young man and the world was very beautiful and glorious.

Then he arose and went to where the seven big chiefs

2

sat before their tepees, smoking their long red pipes in profound silence; for they were men who saw far. Then he raised his voice and spoke to the chiefs.

"Fathers, give Mun-chpe the eagle feather to wear; for has he not touched and slain a big chief, fighting so closely that he breathed the breath of his enemy?"

A swift light passed into the stolid faces of the council, then died out, and stern justice made their faces cold. Again the youth spoke.

"Fathers, give Mun-chpe the eagle feather that men may know him as a brave man."

Then the big medicine man, Wa-zhing-a Sa-ba himself, laid down his pipe and spoke.

"Wa-sa-ba Tun-ga says he killed the big chief; many times he has seen the Hunga Mubli, when the snows drift against the Hungas; he is an old man; Mun-chpe is a young man."

With a grunt of suspicion he ceased speaking. Then Mun-chpe spoke, impetuously, after the manner of youth.

"Fathers, may the thunder strike Mun-chpe; may the buffalo bulls horn him in the hunt; may the wolves devour his bones if he lies! Mun-chpe killed the big chief; give him the eagle feather that men may know he is brave!"

Then Wa-zhing-a Sa-ba spoke: "Wa-kunda is a wise god; Wakunda will help the truthful. Bring the otter skin, and summon Wa-sa-ba Tun-ga that we may know who lies."

The otter skin was brought. It was a hide, down the

3

back of which a piece of grooved wood was fastened. This was considered a holy relic and was used in deciding the truthfulness of disputants. Each of the disputants was to hold an arrow above his head at arm's length, dropping it at the groove. If Wakunda caused the arrow to fall in the groove, then he who dropped it was truthful.

Wa-sa-ba Tun-ga and Mun-chpe took places before the holy relic, and the second, raising the arrow high over his head, prayed aloud: "Wakunda pity Mun-chpe. Wakunda, help Mun-chpe!" Then he dropped the arrow. With a cry, he fled from the sight. The arrow had fallen away from the groove. Rushing into his tepee he buried his face in a buffalo robe and wept, moaning "Wakunda lies; who will tell the truth?" The thought drove him mad. What! Wakunda who moulded the glorious brown prairies! Wakunda who made the great bright sun! Wakunda who put the song in the bird's throat! Wakunda lie! The thought was terrible, for Mun-chpe was a young man.

Now, Wa-te-na would not be his squaw! Maybe she would go to the lodge of Wa-sa-ba Tun-ga! The thought bit him like a poisoned arrow shot by a strong man.

All night he wept in his lodge, moaning, "Wah-hoo-ha-a, Wah-hoo-ha-a," the exclamation of sorrow. And the thunder men, awakened from their sleep by the moaning of Mun-chpe, trembled as they crept closer under their blankets, saying, "Wa-kunda is punishing Mun-chpe; it is a bad thing to lie." Then they shut out the sound with their blankets, and slept again.

But Mun-chpe did not sleep. No! He would not sleep

until he had seen the blood of Wa-sa-ba Tun-ga's breast. Until then he would not sleep. And till the dawn crept in through the chinks in his tepee he moaned and cried for revenge.

Some hours later he was roused from his brooding by shouting and the gallop of ponies. Creeping to the door of his lodge he pushed back the flap and looked out. There was a long line of braves, decked in their brightest colors, with eagle feathers in their hair, urging their ponies about the circle of the village, shouting their war cries.

A tall cottonwood pole had been placed erect in front of the lodge of the council, where the seven chiefs sat glorying in the prowess of the young men. As the braves rode at full gallop past the pole, they discharged their arrows and spears at a dead eagle which was fastened to the top. In all possible manners they rode, hanging by their bare legs to the pony and shooting under his belly and beneath his neck, combining feats of marksmanship with feats of riding. Mun-chpe noted the applause of the old men when an arrow quivered in the breast of the eagle; and oh, how he longed to try his skill!

But, ah! There rode Wa-sa-ba Tung-a, mounted upon a fleeter pony than the rest, dashing at a full run! As he drew near to the pole he stood up on the back of his plunging steed and hurled three arrows in swift succession into the breast of the eagle. The beholders went mad with delight, but Mun–chpe crept back into his tepee, for his heart was fierce within him; he had seen his eagle feather on the head of Wa-sa-ba Tung-a!

The day passed; but Mun-chpe did not appear. As the evening came on, the southeast grew black with storm clouds, and with the fall of the night the wind and rain burst howling upon the village. The thunder shouted and the lightning glared like the eyes of an angry man, but it was sweet to the heart of Mun-chpe, for it seemed that the elements were angry with him. He laughed when the fierce light leaped into the lodge; and he was glad to hear the groaning of the poles; it was like the voice of a brother!

When the night was late he took his knife and went out into the storm. He knew where Wa-sa-ba slept among the Hungas; and thither he ran. Raising the flap of his enemy's tepee, he saw, by the glare of the lightning, Wa-sa-ba sleeping. With the step of a mountain lion he crept to the side of his foe. He knew where to strike. Wa-sa-ba would not cry out. Carefully he pulled the robe from the bare breast, and waited for the lightning. The knife found his enemy's heart. The dying man groaned.

"Hi hi," Mun-chpe cried to himself. "Wa-sa-ba will not need the eagle feather now. Mun-chpe will wear his eagle feather now!"

He snatched the coveted trophy from the dead man's head, and rushed out into the storm, shouting "Hia, hia!" back at the thunder. Then he went into his tepee, and wrapping himself in his blankets, slept. It was so sweet to kill!

But at that time of the morning when scarcely the flight of an arrow could be discerned, a spirit came into Mun-chpe's dream. Its eyes were like two cold flames that dance in a swamp; but its face was Wa-sa-ba Tun-ga's, drawn with the last pang of death! Dolefully the spirit moaned, putting its clammy face against the face of Mun-chpe—its blue lips against the lips of Mun-chpe! It seemed to be drinking his breath. And oh, the eyes! Gasping, the dreamer shrieked and leaped to his feet; and there, outside his lodge, in the glad light of the morning, he beheld the seven stern chiefs of the council, peering in at him.

He knew what they had come to say, for it was forbidden to a murderer that he remain within the circle of the village. Proudly he threw back his head and folded his arms.

"Fathers, Mun-chpe is ready," he said, and he followed them to the council lodge.

When the dusk of the evening came, the village was out to witness the ejection of the murderer. Wrapped in a buffalo robe, so that his face alone was visible, Mun-chpe was driven with the lash about the circle of his people for the last time. But suddenly his eyes lit up with a wild glory, as he saw, standing with her father and mother before their lodge, Wa-te-na!

As he passed her he cried softly, "Wa-te-na, Wa-te-na," and as he was driven on by his guards, he heard a low plaintive sob, and his heart grew lighter within him.

Mun-chpe was driven out of the opening to the east, and there the jeering crowd stopped; but he could not stop; he must go out into the night—out on the desolate prairie alone!

The shouting of the crowd died out, and the night was

very dark and lonely. When the night was old he grew weary, and climbing to the top of a hill, he lifted his voice and cried, "O Wakunda, pity Mun-chpe!" He listened as though expecting to hear an answer. He could hear a far-away pack of coyotes yelp among the hills, ending in a long, dirge-like howl. The sound terrified him, for it seemed the dying groan of Wa-sa-ba Tung-a! Mad with fright he looked behind him into the darkness. There were the two flaming eyes and the drawn, set face of the dead man, with parted lips that jeered at him while they moaned! Wildly shrieking, he turned and dashed down the hill, running, running, running from that hateful face behind him. He ran, until with exhaustion he fell; and there in his delirious dream he could hear the moan and see the terrible glowing eyes, until the big fair dawn leaped above the hills and wakened him. Then he arose and wandered on toward the sunrise.

A sense of terrible loneliness seized him. The limitless prairies were desolate and brown, for it was near on to the time when "the elk break their antlers" (October), and he shivered as he thought of the nearness of "Hunga Mub-li," (December), the time when the snows drift from the north. As the day passed he grew very hungry, and he looked lovingly at his bow, the one thing dear left him in his loneliness.

The night came down, and the wolves yelped and howled in the darkness. But Mun-chpe was hungry, and hunger is fearless. He stealthily hurried toward the sound of the wolves; and creeping on hands and knees down a ravine skirted with plum thickets he could see their glaring eyes and hear the gnashing of their teeth. Fitting an arrow to his bow, he aimed it between the lurid eyes of a beast as it sat upon its haunches, howling. The bow string twanged; the arrow shrieked like the voice of a dying squaw. The wolf, with a mournful howl, leaped in the air and fell back moaning; and as Mun-chpe looked and listened, the moan was the dying moan of Wa-sa-ba Tung-a, and there arose from the quivering carcass that terrible pair of eyes—that drawn, set face with its frozen leer!

Mun-chpe fell on his face in terror. When he looked again, the vision was gone, and he ran to the dead animal, hurriedly tearing away the skin and devouring the meat ravenously. Then he lay down and slept a heavy sleep. In his dream Wa-te-na came to him with out-stretched arms, weeping, "Come back, Mun-chpe, come back to Wa-te-na," she moaned. He awoke, and the pale dawn was on the hills.

Many suns passed and Mun-chpe wandered alone on the prairies, longing for his home and Wa-te-na, and he said to himself, "I will go closer to the village, that I may hear the braves sing, as they dance about the fires!"

But the north wind awoke, and the snow scurried through the short buffalo grass, and Mun-chpe was weak from hunger. The sharp gusts crept under his buffalo robe and stung his bare legs. When he came in sight of the village it was evening. He waited for the night, and then crept close to the tepees and heard the old men talk. Oh, if he could sit with them by the crackling logs and hear their stories. Never, never, could he do this again. He was as the coyote that howls for loneliness among the frozen hills and dies of hunger.

With a sigh he turned away from the sight and set his face against the storm, for he wished to die.

"Wa-hoo-ha-a, wa-hoo-ha-a," he cried.

The old men heard the cry blown upon the storm, and they told weird tales that made the staring youths shudder.

That night Wa-te-na, sleeping in the lodge of her father, had a dream. It seemed to her that Mun-chpe came to her and his body was gaunt and weak, and his eyes were wild and fierce like a hungry wolf's. "Wa-te-na," she heard him say, imploringly, "Wa-te-na." She awoke, and wrapping her blankets about her went out into the storm.

She could hear the faint cry of anguish in the distance, and she hurried toward the cry.

"Wah-hoo-ha-a-a, wah-hoo-ha-a-a," tremulously came the wail through the storm, and soon Wa-te-na stumbled upon the form of Mun-chpe.

She rubbed his face and hands, striving to warm them; but the body grew colder. Then she covered him with her blanket and pressed her body close to his, her lips close to the frozen lips.

Some time afterward, a party searching for the lost Wa-te-na, found her frozen body outstretched upon the cold form of Mun-chpe. And to this day the old women tell their daughters of the devotion of Wa-te-na. But the name of Mun-chpe is not spoken.

Overland Monthly, August 1901

The Singing of the Frogs

Wabisgaha loved the tawny stretches of the prairie smiling like a rugged, honest face under the kiss of the sunlight; he loved the storm that frowned and shouted like an angry chief; he loved the southwind and the scent of the spring, yet the love of woman he knew not, for his heart was given to his horse, Ingla Hota, which means Laughing Thunder.

Why should he have a squaw? Did not Laughing Thunder toss his mane and neigh when he heard the soft steps of his master? Was not Laughing Thunder his companion and his helpmeet? Ah, no, Wabisgaha would have no squaw.

And furthermore, his love for Laughing Thunder was not sentiment; it was religion. Many and weird were the tales that the wise old men told about the evening fires concerning the horse of Wabisgaha. It was said in a subdued voice, lest that some demon face should peer into the circle of the fire from the darkness, that Laughing Thunder contained an evil spirit; that Wabisgaha was secretly a great medicine man, who had learned the terrible words that tame the spirits of the thunder, and had made the black Power of the storm come down and be his horse. Yes, and there was one who had watched Laughing Thunder graze all day upon the hills and never a blade was nipped; but where the breath of his nostrils passed, the grass was seared as with lightning. Another had noticed how Laughing Thunder wasted away when the storms were few, like sunflowers pining for the rain; and how one night when the lightning flashed and the thunder howled, he had seen a burning horse leap from the top of a hill and gallop through the clouds, neighing half like the laugh of a man, half like the shout of the thunder.

"Some day Wabisgaha will ride to the land of the spirits," they would all agree, gazing wide-eyed at each other while the last blue flame struggled in the embers. Then they would shrug their shoulders as though the touch of an invisible hand chilled them; shaking their heads by which to say, "Ugh! there are many strange things."

It was the month of the sunflower. Wabisgaha one night, half asleep in his tepee, was aroused by a strange sound among the horses, which were left to graze upon the hills near the village. Creeping out of his tepee into the open air, he could hear nothing but the slumberous moan of the distant thunder, for the southeast was black and glaring by fits with a coming storm. Then there burst forth upon the dull sultry air of the night a shrill, clear neigh and the sound of many hurrying hoofs. That neigh! Ah, it was the neigh of Laughing Thunder. It came again, but this time dimmer, and the gallop of hoofs grew softer as with distance.

Wabisgaha rushed out into the night crying, "Ingla Hota, Ingla Hota." But for answer the storm howled on the hills. By the glare of the lightning he found the trail of the fleeing hoofs. He would take the trail and find his horse. "Ingla Hota, Ingla Hota," he cried. The big rain drops drummed upon the hills. It seemed to him that the thunder cried back, and ended with a sound like the neigh of a mighty steed. So all night he followed the trail of the hoofs southward, mingling his cries with the cries of the wind and the thunder; and when the storm lulled and the day dawned, he climbed to the top of a hill and scanned the drenched prairies, but no horse! Only the pathless brown sea of grass glinting in the sun; a maddening monotony, save for the occasional gulch like a battle-scar on the face of a warrior. No sound except the caw of a distant crow and the monotone of silence.

With a grunt of despair he again took up the trail. He noted that the trail was narrow and well beaten. Horses of themselves do not travel single file. Then he knew that he was following a party of warriors. In his haste he had not take his bow, and his feet were bare to the cactus and prickly pear; yet all day long he kept upon the trail, and when night came he slept upon it. Ah, no, he would not lose Laughing Thunder. Another night passed, and when the sun of the next day was half way down from the zenith, Wabisgaha, standing upon a hill, gazed into the sandy valley of the broad and shallow stream, and there in the wooded bottoms were the jumbled mud lodges of the Pawnee village.

From time unknown the Pawnees and Omahas were friends; yet as Wabisgaha gazed down upon the village he feared that the ancient friendship had been broken. But he was very weary, and the thought of losing Laughing Thunder was like a lash of buckskin behind him. So he passed down into the valley. A band of shouting Pawnees in war paint came out to meet the lone stranger. Several of the party seized upon him, binding his arms behind him with thongs of rawhide, while the others danced deliriously about, shouting and waving their weapons above their heads. And the captive, weary and unarmed, without resistance was led in among the lodges.

There has ever been a something appealingly majestic about the defiance of an Indian; and as Wabisgaha strode beside his captors, naked but for the buckskin breech-clout, decorated with colored beads, his broad chest brown as of beaten copper; the great muscles expanding in impotent anger; the laboring of the lungs; the flash of the black eye from beneath the heavy brow; the long wiry hair tossing on his bare shoulders; these would have suggested to an esthetic imagination the incarnate spirit of the untamed prairies.

As he passed between the rows of shouting Pawnees, he failed to notice among a bunch of squaws an Indian girl who stared at him, wide-mouthed with interest and wonder. She was clad more brilliantly than her companions, and the blue spot upon her forehead at once marked her as a maiden of distinction. It was Umba

(Sunlight), the daughter of the stern warchief of the Pawnees, Pedavashaloo.

As the captive and the captors hurried on to the lodge of the big chief, Umba gazed longingly after them with that soft light in her eye which is not starlight nor sunshine, but has something of the gentle tenderness of the one and the potent glory of the other. A woman is a woman, though her face be angular and swarthy, and the love of a daughter of the prairie takes unto itself an element of boundlessness like the plain and of fury like the winds that sweep.

Umba was moved by the defiant attitude of the captive, for womankind loves bravery. She was charmed by the magnificent brown limbs, the powerful chest, the fierce eye.

Wabisgaha was taken before Pedavashaloo, who stood at the door of his lodge. The bold eye of the captive met the stern glance of the chief, and for a while both were silent. Then the chief spoke:

"Why do you come among my people?"

The captive threw back his head, and in a fierce gutteral, said:

"My people and your people have been friends; your people stole Wabisgaha's horse; give him back that Wabisgaha may return in peace to his village."

The eye of the chief flashed with sudden anger.

"My people do not steal!" he thundered. "My people make war; you are a captive; to-morrow you shall die!"

That night the women who slept in the lodge of Umba were often awakened by her moaning. She was think-

ing of Wabisgaha. But he, lying bound and guarded, did
not moan; he was thinking of his horse. Now he was
going to the land of the spirits. How lonely he would be
without Laughing Thunder. Often through the night he
prayed to Wakunda that his horse might be killed and go
with him. When the sky paled with the early morning he
slept and dreamed. He stood upon a high hill and the
clouds were about him. The feverish red sun was sinking
below him. Suddenly the clouds glowed as when a prairie fire roars and crackles through the night, and then
there burst upon his ear a mighty neigh, half laugh, half
thunder, and a burning steed galloped through the parting mist toward him. He awoke, and the Dawn looked in
at the door! It was a good omen; he would not be afraid to
die. When the sun was scarcely an arrow length above the
hills he was led out from among the lodges into the open
valley.

The whole village trooped behind him, shouting and
mad with expectation, for it was great fun to behold a
captive dragged at the heels of a horse. The rabble grew
thicker as he advanced. A band of shrieking squaws
pushed their way to him and spit in his face. Many times
he was dragged backward by his long hair onto the
sand by the frenzied warriors. All this was borne with a
dogged patience by the captive, for was he not going to
the land of the spirits?

It was an ancient custom among the Pawnees that if a
captive should receive a morsel of meat from one of the
tribe he was to be spared, as thus being favored by the
Great Spirit.

Suddenly the shouting ceased, and the tall imperious form of Pedavashaloo was seen pushing a way through the rabble. Behind him a young squaw followed, carrying a morsel of meat in her hand. Rushing up to the surprised captive, she put the meat to his mouth. Wabisgaha seized and ate the meat greedily, and for the first and last time looked with kindness into the appealing eyes of Umba.

Then a great change came over the multitude. The warriors, but a moment before thirsting for the blood of the captive, now fell back in awe as though the hand of Umba had been the visible hand of the Great Spirit.

Dumb with amazement Wabisgaha stared about him, until Pedavashaloo motioned him to follow; and in silence they took their way to the big chief's lodge. After they had sat down, the chief took two long pipes, and lighting both, handed one to Wabisgaha. Silently they smoked the pipe of peace.

After a while Pedavashaloo spoke, bluntly, after the manner of the prairie: "Umba weeps for Wabisgaha. Come back in the month when the frogs sing (April) and take her for your squaw!"

Then Wabisgaha said: "I will come back in the month when the frogs sing and take her for my squaw. Give me my horse that I may go back to my people."

"Pedavashaloo will feed the horse with his own hand until Wabisgaha comes," the chief answered.

The next morning a band of Pawnees rode out of the village, and among them rode Wabisgaha; but he was not riding Laughing Thunder.

Until noon the band attended him across the prairies; then they turned backward, and alone Wabisgaha rode mournfully northward toward the village of his people.

In the absence of Wabisgaha strange rumors had grown among his tribe concerning him and his horse. The wise old men whispered strange things about the demon horse and its rider. Ah, yes, Wabisgaha had at last ridden to the land of the Thunder Spirits. And the listening youths crept into their blankets very closely at night, dreaming weird dreams.

So when Wabisgaha rode his jaded pony sullenly over the brown brow of the hill and entered the village his people had no cry of welcome for his ears; but slunk away in fear and awe. For had he not been to the land of the thunder spirits? Day by day Wabisgaha sat alone in his lodge, brooding bitterly over the loss of his horse. And the winter swept down from the north and howled across the prairies. Far southward in the village of the Pawnees Umba sat in her lodge and gazed long hours into the crackling fire. There was no winter in her dreaming. She was thinking of the time when the frogs sing, for then she would be the squaw of Wabisgaha.

Many days passed, but Wabisgaha did not leave his lodge, and his people began to wonder, for no one knew in what manner he procured wood for his fire. Then it was rumored about that the thunder spirits dwelt with him in his lodge. Yes, for one whose curiosity led him one night to creep up to the strange man's door had heard him muttering busily with his eyes upon the fire. Yet he was alone.

So it happened one night in the stormy month when the lone goose flies (February) that he was summoned before the seven chiefs of the council. In their great tepee they sat, cross-legged, about the fire. Wabisgaha stood before them, and as they gazed upon his face, they shuddered with fear, for it was the face of a sick man's dream, and the eyes were cold but glowing, for he had mourned much and eaten little.

Then one of the chiefs spoke as one who speaks to a spectre:

"Where did Wabisgaha go in the month of the sunflowers?" (August).

Then Wabisgaha's silence passed, for he could speak of Laughing Thunder. He told them how the Pawnees had stolen his horse; how he had followed the trail to their village; how they would have slain him but for the gift of a morsel of meat. He spoke with all the eloquence of a wronged man and with all the pathos of a simple heart that is wounded. But the seven chiefs were silent. They feared him and doubted his story. After talking together for some time, they again spoke to him:

"If Wabisgaha has been wronged, we will give him revenge. He shall lead a war party against the Pawnees, but he must not return alive!"

So Wabisgaha withdrew to his lodge. All night he brooded by his fire. Why should he have a squaw? He would lead a war party against the Pawnees. He would have revenge for the stealing of Laughing Thunder. A great, wild happiness came over him; after that he went about the village with a glad heart and his people ceased to fear him.

One morning, in the time when the frogs sing, the war party started southward, and Wabisgaha rode at their head. All day their ponies scurried across the green hills. All night they rode, and long before the east was gray they halted upon the hill that overlooked the valley of the broad and shallow stream where the Pawnee village nestled.

At the time when the flight of an arrow could be discerned, Wabisgaha rode in front of his band, and, dismounting, he raised his eyes to the gray heavens and uttered his last prayer to Wakunda. Then he seized a handful of dust and tossed it above his head. Thus a brave ever does before going to certain death. Then he mounted his pony, and, with a terrible yell, the war party swooped down the hill into the sleeping village. The Pawnees could make but little resistance, and those who were not slain fled in terror, followed by the frenzied Omahas. But Wabisgaha did not ride in pursuit. His knife was red with revenge, and now he would die!

Some distance from him he beheld the tall form of Pedavashaloo standing before his lodge in defiance. His arms and breast were besmeared with the blood of the Omahas who lay in a semi-circle about him. His long, sinewy arms were corded with the stress of fight, and his hand clasped the terrible hunting knife.

Wabisgaha cast away his bow and quiver of arrows, and dismounting, he took his knife in his hand, and,

raising his arms to the skies, he uttered a low wail four
times. Then he rushed at the defiant chief. There was
none to see the struggle, for the clamor of the fight came
dimly from far down the valley, and the muffled wail of
the women was heard from the lodges. Each knife found
a bare, brown breast, and side by side the enemies lay,
choking, until their spirits passed into the happy land
where the tribes are at peace.

That night, amid the silence of the stricken village,
Umba crept from among the terrified women, and, hurrying to where Laughing Thunder was staked by the
lodge of her father, she led the horse to where the body of
Wabisgaha lay among her dead kinsmen. With great
effort she placed the body across the horse's back, and,
taking a bow and arrow from one of the dead warriors,
she mounted behind the body and rode off into the still,
clear night of the prairies.

After riding many hours, she dismounted in a valley
and placed the body on the ground. Then fitting the
arrow to the string of the bow, she sent it into the heart
of Laughing Thunder. Now Wabisgaha would find his
horse in the land of the spirits. Then Umba sat beside the
bodies and moaned.

The night passed and the sun looked over the green
hills into the valley and found Umba watching by the
bodies. All that day she waited, singing softly a wild
Indian song to the spirit of Wabisgaha. And the crows
came out of the horizon in a low trailing cloud, cawing in
anticipation of their meal. Umba kept them away by
shaking her robe above her head and singing louder.

Then the crows, with a dismal rustle of wings, would soar above the three, cawing clamorously. The evening came and the frogs sang in the valley. Yes, it was the time of the singing of the frogs. This was the time when she should have become the squaw of Wabisgaha. Plaintively she moaned at the thought, gazing upon the pinched face beside her. The night fell, and Umba was very faint with hunger and watching. So she laid her head upon the breast of Wabisgaha. Maybe she would wake and be with him in the land of the spirits.

The night passed, and when the sun looked into the valley, Umba was lying motionless where she had lain down to sleep.

The crows swooped down, chattering; they were not frightened away.

Months afterward a hunting party of Omahas, finding upon the prairie three skeletons, one of a squaw, one of a buck, and one of a horse, returned to the tribe and told a story at the evening fires.

But they could not know how Wabisgaha died for his horse and Umba died for Wabisgaha.

Overland Monthly, September 1901

The Triumph of Seha

When Seha had grown to be a tall youth, he said to the old men: "Now I am almost a man; what shall I do?" For being a youth, he dreamed of great things. And the old men answered: "That Wakunda knows; therefore, take yourself to a high hill; there fast and pray until sleep comes, and with it a vision."

So Seha arose and laid aside his garments, and naked, went out on the prairie. When he had gone far, he climbed to the top of a lonely hill, bare of grass and strewn with flakes of stone that made its summit white like the head of a man who has seen many winters.

Then he knelt upon the flinty summit, and raising his palms to the heavens, he cried: "O Wakunda, here needy stands Seha!" Four times he uttered the cry, yet there was no sound save that of the crow overhead, and the wind in the short grass of the hillside.

Then he fell into an agony of weeping, and wetting his palms with his tears, he rubbed them in the white dust and smeared his face with mud. Then he cast his wet eyes to the heavens, and again raised his hands in supplication.

"O Wakunda, Seha is a young man; he would do great things like the old men; send him a vision!"

The night came down and still he held his eyes upon the darkening heavens, crying for a vision. But only the coyote answered him. The stars looked out of the east and steadily climbed upward, gazing upon his tearful face. But when the grey of age began to grow upon the forehead of the Night, he grew so weary that he fell forward upon his face and slept.

And lo! the vision came!

It seemed that the skies were black and fierce as the face of a brave in anger. The lightning glared; and the thunder shouted like a warrior in the front of the battle! Then the cloud split, and through it rushed a mighty eagle with the lightning playing on its wings; its cry was like the shriek of a dying foe and its eyes were bright with the vision that sees far. Its wings hovered over Seha, and it spoke:

"Seha shall be a seer of things far off. His thought shall be quick as the lightning, and his voice shall be as thunder in the ears of men!"

Seha awoke, and he was shivering with the dews of morning. Then he arose and walked back toward his village, slowly, for his thoughts were great. Four days he went about the village, speaking to no one; and the people whispered: "Seha has had a vision; do you not see that his eyes are big with a strange light?"

One night after the four days had passed, Seha arose from his blankets and, creeping stealthily out of his te-pee, he went to the lodge of Ebahamba, who has a great medicine-man, for Seha wished to tell his vision into a wise ear.

Pulling back the buffalo robe that hung across the entrance he saw the great man sleeping in the moonlight that fell through the opening at the top of the tepee. Entering, he touched the shoulder of the sleeper, who awoke with a start, and, sitting up, stared at the young intruder. Then Ebahamba being thoroughly awakened, spoke:

"Seha has come to tell his vision; I knew he would come; speak."

"You are a great man," began Seha, "and your eyes are like the sun's eyes to see into the shadow. Hear me and teach me."

Then he told of his vision on the lonely hill.

As Ebahamba listened to the wonderful thing that had befallen the youth, his heart grew cold with envy; for certainly great things were in store for Seha, and might it not come to pass that the youth should grow even greater in power than Ebahamba himself?

So, when the youth had ceased, breathless with the wonder of the thing he told, the old man said coldly: "Wakunda will teach Seha; let him go learn of the wind and the growing things!"

Then the youth arose and left the lodge. But the big medicine-man slept no more that night, for jealousy is sleepless.

At that time it happened that the winds were hot from the southwest, and the maize grew yellow as the sun that smote it, and the rainless air curled its blades. And the old man Ebahamba cried to Wakunda for rain; but the skies only glared back for answer.

Then a great moan went up before the lodge of the big medicine-man, Ebahamba. "Ebahamba speaks with the spirits; let him pray to the thunder spirits that we may have food for our squaws and our children!"

And Ebahamba shut himself in his tepee four days, fasting, crying to the thunder spirits, and performing strange rites. But every morning the sun arose glaring like the eye of a man who dies of fever, and the hot wind sweltered up from the southwest, moaning hoarsely like one who moans with thirst; and the maize heard the moan and wilted.

Then when the people grew clamorous before the lodge of Ebahamba, he came forth and said: "The thunder spirits are sleeping; they are weary and drowsy with the heat." And the hooting of his people drove him back into his lodge.

Then Seha raised his voice above the despairing murmur of the village, saying: "Seha is a young man, yet the thunder spirits will hear him, be they ever so drowsy, for Seha has had a vision. Seha will call the rain."

The murmur of the people ceased, for so strange a light was in the eyes of the youth that they believed.

"Let Seha give us rain," they cried, "and he shall be a great man among his people!"

Then Seha strode out of the village and disappeared in the hills. His heart was loud as he walked, for would he not be a great man among his people? He believed in his power with that belief which *is* the power. All day he walked, and when the red sun glared across the western hills like an eye bloodshot with pain, he came to a clump of cottonwoods that sang upon the summit of a bluff.

Now the thunder spirits love the cottonwoods, for they rise sternly from the earth, reaching their long arms into the clouds, and they cry back at the storm with a loud voice. Where the cottonwood sings, there the thunder spirits sleep, and the thunder birds, the eagle and the hawk, watch with keen eyes.

Under the trees Seha stood, and raising his hands and his eyes to the heavens, he cried: "Hear Seha! For is he not a thunder man? Did he not dream the thunder man's dream? Then I command you, send the big clouds boiling before the wind; send the rains, that my people may have food for their children. Then I will be a great man among my people!"

The trees only tossed their branches above him, while they sang softly in the wind.

"O Thunder Spirits!" he cried again. "You are not asleep! I hear you talking together in the tree tops. Listen to me, for I am a thunder man!"

Then a dead calm grew. The cottonwoods were still. Suddenly they groaned with a cool gust from the east. The groan was like a waking man's groan when he arises, stretching and yawning, from his blankets.

Then Seha lay down to sleep; for were not the thunder spirits awake?

When the night was late, Seha was awakened by the howl of the thunder. He saw the quick lightning pierce the boiling darkness in the east. Then the rain drops danced upon the dry hills with a sound like the unintelligible patter of many voices that are glad.

Seha was glad, and he answered the shout of the thunder. His people in the village were glad, and their tongues were noisy with the name of Seha. The maize was glad and it looked up to the kind sky, tossing its arms in exultation.

When Seha returned to the village, he was the centre of a joyful cry; he had become a great man among his people. And when they asked from whence he had such great powers, he said: "I caught it from the blowing wind; I heard it in the growing of the maize."

But there was one who did not greet the mysterious youth. Ebahamba shut himself in his tepee, for had he not failed to awaken the thunder spirits when a youth had succeeded? Ebahamba sat sullenly in his tepee, thinking great and fierce thoughts; and after many days of fasting, his magic came back to him. Then he summoned to his lodge one by one, the men of his band, and he said to each: "Behold! Seha speaks with evil spirits. May he not destroy his people? Then let us perform the rite of *Wazhinadee* against him that he may be forsaken by man and beast and so die!"

The men of his band believed Ebahamba, for his magic was very great now, and he forced them to believe. So each man went to his tepee, shut himself in, feasted and thought sternly against Seha. For this is the manner of the rite of *Wazhinadee*.

Then after his enemies had thought strongly for many days against him, Seha was seized with a strange weakness. His eyes lost their brightness, and he could not see far as before. All through the days and the nights he went about the village, crying for his lost power; and the people said: "The coyotes are barking in the hills." They could not see him for the mist that the terrible rite had cast about him.

Then Seha wandered out on the prairie, wailing as ever for his lost power. And after many days he laid himself down by a stream to die. But he did not die. He slept; and the vision came again. When he awoke, he was strong again and his eyes could see far as before.

Then he said: "I will cleanse myself in the stream and go back to my people, for I am strong again."

But lo! as he leaned over the clear stream, he beheld the reflected image of an eagle far above him. Now a medicine man can change himself at will into anything that walks or crawls or flies or is still; and as Seha watched the eagle, he knew that it was Ebahamba!

So gliding into the stream, he quickly changed himself into a great fish floundering temptingly upon the surface. The eagle, which was Ebahamba, being hungry, swooped down upon the fish with wide beak and open talons.

In a moment, Seha changed himself into a huge boulder, against which the swooping bird dashed furiously, crushing its beak and talons. Then it arose, and with bloody wings, fluttered across the prairie.

Seha stepped out of his rock and laughed a loud, long laugh, and the eagle, which was Ebahamba, heard and knew.

So Seha returned to his village and was a great man among his people. But Ebahamba hid himself in his tepee; and a rumour ran that his arms were broken and his face crushed.

And there was much wonder in the village!

Overland Monthly, October 1901

The Spirit of Crow Butte

Should a European fashion a personification of Martyr-
dom, it would have a white face. This is a reproach to the
blind egotism of individual races.

There is a story that the old bucks tell to the staring
youths huddled about the winter fires, which is a simple
plea for the brotherhood of humanity pale and swarthy.
A noble deed has many whispering tongues, and becomes a part of nature like the wind, and the Omaha
from whom I had this simple legend knew not whence it
came; it had crept into the varied tongues of the scattered
tribes to be an incentive to their youths.

On the desolate plains of Western Nebraska there rises
from the banks of the White River a steep butte of clay
and sandstone. Should one take the winding path, by
which alone it can be scaled, and clamber to its summit,
he would be terrified by the loneliness of the place, with
its sun-bleached boulders and its moaning pines. Upon
all sides, save where the tortuous path struggles upward,
the yellow butte drops almost vertically to the sandy
plain dotted with bunch grass, that sweeps off on all sides

in a level, unbroken stretch to where the pure blue sky dims the vision; to the very gates of night and day. One sitting there could not but believe that there, at least, Time forgets its fever and sleeps. There is a spell upon the place, and the wind, the crow and the coyote make the only sounds that break it.

Many summers ago, when the white man to the Indian was yet a name that dwelt in the mysterious regions of the rising sun, a small band of Crows came scurrying across these prairies, followed by a larger band of Sioux. There was little hope for the Crows, for their ponies were jaded with a recent buffalo hunt, and the Sioux steadily gained upon them. But a cry of joy went up from the hard-pressed band as they beheld the one rugged way leading to the summit of the butte. Here was momentary safety, at least. So dismounting at the foot of the butte, which a horse could not climb, they barely had time to send an arrow into the heart of each weary pony, and rush up the steep path, before the Sioux were upon them, howling in their baffled anger.

There was no further pursuit. A small band once in possession of the butte could hold it with ease against a horde of warriors. Yet there was a greater, grimmer enemy awaiting them upon that desolate summit. Starvation was there, and the awful torture of thirst beneath the glare of a prairie sun!

When the small band had clambered to the top, they turned and looked below. There they beheld their enemies making ready to camp at the foot of the path. They

looked about them and saw death grinning in the desolation of the shelterless summit, strewn with its bare
rocks, where the hardy soap weed could scarcely struggle upward.

Before them was the torture of thirst and hunger,
behind them the more terrible torture of the Sioux, and
they knew their enemies too well to hope for their with-
drawal from the foot of the butte.

The day passed, and the sun dropped suddenly beneath its yellow veil of plain, leaving scarcely a brief twilight in its wake, and the Crows looked wistfully over the
darkening prairie, across which they would never again
urge their fleet ponies in the dusty path of the bison.

When the night fell they made themselves a cheerless
camp, and, gathering twigs from beneath the pine trees,
they built a fire that had no gladness in it. Then, sitting
about the flame that lit up the despair of their swarthy
faces, they held a council.

There was but one way in which the band could be
saved. By cutting their buffalo robes into strips and
binding these together, they could lower themselves,
one by one, to the plain below.

Yet the Sioux were watchful, and would quickly de-
tect their absence, unless some show of fight were kept
up; otherwise, there would be little chance for a small
band on foot to flee before the well-mounted Sioux. So it
was decided that someone must remain upon the butte to
keep the fires burning and to hurl an occasional arrow
or stone into the enemy's camp, until the fleeing band
should be beyond vision.

Who would die upon the butte to save his band? To remain meant death.

The desperate Crows sat and gazed questioningly at each other through the weird glare of the flame, and, save for the wail of the pines, there was silence. In his own rude and picturesque manner an Indian loves his home, his squaw, and his brown-faced papooses; but more than these he loves the freedom of the plains, the dash of the hunt, the ecstasy of fight—all that is unrestrained he loves. It were easy for him to die with the shout of the foe in his ears; for this requires animal fury rather than courage. But to suffer the slow, inglorious death of starvation and thirst upon a lonely butte, whence he could gaze, like one disinherited, upon his broad free plains—this was hard.

So each stared at the other while the pines groaned piteously like a starving man, and the uncertain fire made the darkness weird.

But suddenly, out of the painful silence, a voice spoke:

"I am a young man," it began hoarsely, as though issuing from a throat at which a cold, invisible hand was clutching.

The warriors raised their eyes from staring at the flames, and sought the circle of anguished faces where the firelight danced. They saw the face of a youth made terrible with anguish and the shadow. The lips quivered with unspoken words, and in the eyes a cold terror glittered.

"I am a young man," the voice continued; and it seemed the articulate sorrow of the wind. "My home is

35

sweet to me; I love to hear the women crooning to the children. I shall never hear them croon to mine. I love to watch the dancing of the braves. I shall never dance with them again. The growing maize sings sweetly in the summer winds. There is one whose ears shall be dumb."

The voice wailed into silence like a fitful night wind, and the listening braves shivered with a vague terror. They knew the meaning of the young man's words.

The band arose, and over the youth performed the strange rites for the dead. Then they fell to constructing a rope of their blankets. They worked swiftly and silently; but the young man stared distractedly into the blaze, and his face was the face of a corpse, animated with terror. Did some broad, brown face weave itself amid the fantastic leapings of the flame, that he gazed so intently? Did the crackling of the burning twigs sing to him of the merry camp fires of his people?

Suddenly he raised his eyes from the embers and looked about him. He was alone! Then an overpowering sense of loneliness rushed upon him.

Running to the edge of the butte, he found the rope of buffalo hide hanging from a jutting ledge and swaying in the night wind.

He strained his ears to catch some faint echo of farewell from fleeing footsteps.

The pines moaned.

He endeavored with painful gaze to form some dim moving shadow from the impenetrable night that swallowed his fleeing brothers.

He shivered with the terror of the dusk.

Then again he found the hanging rope. Should he let himself down and run, run, run out of this weird place where black spirits lurked? With a quick movement, he grasped the rope, and, wrenching it from the ledge, hurled it from him into the darkness!

He was a dead man. A dead man is not afraid of death. He must keep the fires burning, that the Sioux might be outwitted.

So he went back to the lonely fires and replenished them that they leaped far up into the night. But when the stars grew paler with the coming of the dawn, he again stood upon the edge of the butte and scanned the prairie, slowly emerging from the shadow, and saw nothing but the monotonous sweep of yellow plain, hemmed with the faint line of light that forewent the day.

Days passed, and when the Sioux no longer noted signs of life upon the butte, they struck their camp and rode away.

Many times since then the plains have thundered with the bellowing of the bulls. Many times have the snows drifted from the north, and the corrosive seasons have reduced to dust the skeleton of the nameless brave. Yet if you should ride to the place in that mysterious hour when light and shadow struggle and the broad white Day swoops down upon the plain; and should you gaze through the half light of the early morning upon the yellow summit of Crow Butte, you would see, some say, a lonely figure with hand at brow, peering with strained and anxious gaze into the distance. And you would hear a wail like that of a man who dies of thirst and hunger.

The form may be only a sunflower, heavy and bent with seed, clothed in the magic of the shadow.

The wail may be the wail of the pines as the morning winds awaken.

Yet I love to think differently.

Overland Monthly, November 1901

The Beating of the
War Drums

He could never be a strong *waschusha* (brave). When he
was born he was no bigger than a baby coyote littered in
a terrible winter after a summer of famine! That was
what the braves said as they sat in a circle about the fires;
and often one would catch him, spanning his little brown
legs with a contemptuous forefinger and thumb, while
the others made much loud mirth over this bronze mite
who could never be a brave.

Then the object of their mirth would pull away from
his tormentors, displaying his teeth with a whimper
that was half a growl, and would slink away into the
shades where the firelight did not reach. Whereupon the
braves would call after him in their good-natured cruelty: "Mixa Zhinga! Mixa Zhinga!" (Little Wolf).

So, in accordance with certain infallible psychic laws,
Little Wolf became what he was considered, and fulfilled
his wild name to the letter.

One day in one of his most vulpine moods, while
trotting among the hills on all fours, stopping now and
then to sit upon his haunches and give forth a series of
howls in imitation of his namesakes, he had discovered a

deserted wolf's hole in the hillside, of which he immediately made himself the growling possessor.

To make this play metempsychosis the more real,
he had spirited from the tepee of his father a complete
wolf's hide, clad in which he spent the greater part of the
time prowling about among the hills with an intense
wolfish hate for all humankind gnawing at his heart.

One summer evening Little Wolf, sitting upon the top
of the hill, gazed down upon the circle of tepees which
was the village of his people. As he looked, the silent
vow he had taken, never to go back to his tribe again,
but to be a wolf with the wolves, slowly became shape-
less, then indistinct, then it vanished altogether. For the
smoke, rising slowly from the various fires, told a be-
witching tale of supper to his eyes; and the light wind
brought to his keen nostrils the scent of boiling kettles,
which acted as a sort of footnote to the tale of the smoke,
finally clinching the argument of the text!

So the little wolf fell from his high resolve as the wolf
skin fell from his back, and he forthwith trotted down
the hillside, at every step degenerating, as he thought,
into just a common *zhinga zhinga* (baby).

Having cautiously approached a fire, Little Wolf sat
upon the ground with his knees huddled up to his chin,
and watched the deft hands of the women tending the
baking of the squaw corn cakes and the yellow *watuh*
(pumpkin) in the embers.

The old women, their backs bent with their loads,
carried bundles of faggots from a thicket near by and
placed them upon the fires, that flared up with a sound

like the wind's, making a small circular day amid the
gathering shadows. The air was pleasant with the scent
of boiling kettles, some filled with the meat of the *tae* or
the *tachuga* (bison and antelope); some ebullient with the
savoury *zhew munka,* the tea of the prairie. And as Little
Wolf sat and looked upon the suggestive scene, a great
wave of sympathetic kindness passed through his small
body.

And especially did the wolfishness of his little heart
melt into an indefinite feeling of love for humanity as his
eyes followed the form of the maiden Hinnagi as she
bustled with her mother about the kettles. Already in his
childish mind he was wielding the stone axe with mighty
force in some mysterious battle among the hills; and it
was all for her. His eyes grew big with the dream he
was dreaming. He stared into the fire as he thought the
thoughts of ambitious youth.

The flame fell and crept into the embers. Then real-
ity came back as the shadows came. Something of the
wonted wolfishness tugged at his heart as he thought of
what the braves had said. He could never be a strong
brave! With an awful bitterness this thought grew upon
him, and even a full stomach could not quite ease the
pang.

After the evening meal the war drums were brought
into the open space about which the tepees were built.
For upon the morrow the entire band of the tribe's warriors would go out against their enemies, the Sioux, and
to-night they would dance the war dance that their courage might not fail.

The drums were placed in a small circle; before each
an old man, who had seen many battles ere the eagle
glance faded from his eye, sat cross-legged, holding a
drumstick in either hand. About these the braves gathered in a larger circle. The yellow and red light of the
boisterous camp fires made more terrible their faces
fierce with the war paint.

In another circle at some distance from that of the
braves, awaited the women, dressed in their brightest
garments of dyed buckskin. At a signal from the head
chief of the tribe, the snarling thunder of the war drums
began. The two motionless circles suddenly became two
rings of gyrating colour. The beaded moccasins twin-
kled like a chain of satellites swinging about the faggot
fire for a sun. The shout of the braves arose above the
cadence of the drum beats, and the monotonous song of
the women grew like a night wind in a lonesome valley.

Tum-tum-um-um, tum-tum-um-um, went the
drums, ever faster, ever louder, inciting the dancers to
delirious fury. The neglected fires dwindled into embers. The shout of the braves and the droning of the
women ceased. Darkness fell upon the circles. The dancers moved swiftly through the dusk like ghosts in a
midnight orgy. There was no sound save the snarling
beat of the drums and the shuffle of wild feet.

Then the moon, big-eyed with wonder, arose above
the hills, pouring a weird light upon the dance. Little
Wolf, who had been huddling closely against a tepee
with an unintelligible fear, now felt the delirium of the
dance for the first time. He leaped to his feet with a shout

that echoed strange and hoarse from the hills! The whole village, as if awakened from the spell, caught up the cry and sent it trembling up the gulches!

With the hot blood pounding at his temples, Little Wolf swung into the frenzy of the dance. He leaped like the antelope when it catches the scent of the hunter. He was no longer the *zhinga zhinga* who could never be a brave. The fanaticism of the savage was upon him. With his head thrown back until it caught the full glare of the moon, he danced. It was not a child's face that the pale light struck; it was the face of a fiend! The unfettered wind of the prairie was in his lungs! The swiftness of the elk was in his feet! He danced until the hills danced about him in a dance of their own. He danced until the moon reeled like a sick man! He danced until his chest felt crushed as with the hug of a grizzly! He danced until the stars and the moon went out, and there was nothing but darkness and a deep, deep oppressive something, like and unlike slumber, upon him! The sun was far up in the heavens when he awoke lying upon the ground where he had fallen with fatigue. He rubbed his eyes and stared about him; the circles of the dance had vanished; the war drums were still. The warriors had ridden out of the village into the mysterious region beyond the hills where great deeds awaited to be done. Only the women and the children and the old men remained in the village.

Then there came upon Little Wolf that overpowering thought of bitterness. He was only a *zhinga zhinga;* he could never be a brave. No, but he would be a wolf! He would live in howling loneliness among the hills!

Yet that day as he prowled about, clad in his wolf skin, he was conscious of not being half so good a wolf as he had been the day before. He did not find it quite within his power to hate his people with whom he had felt the delirium of the war dance. The snarling beat of the war drums had awakened in him a vital interest in the great prairie tragedy of food-getting and war-making.

Several days passed, and the warriors had not returned. Little Wolf was sitting beside the deserted hole which was his den, thinking great thoughts of the future as he basked in the horizontal glare of the evening sun. As he looked with half-shut eyes across the hills, his dreaming was suddenly arrested by the sight of what seemed a number of bunches of grass moving along the brow of the hill on the other side of the valley in which the village lay. As he looked and wondered at this fantastic dance of the grasses, there was a wild shout from the opposite hill, and a small band of Otoes, their heads covered with grass that they might the more easily creep upon their foes, rushed down the hillside toward the defenseless village.

Terrified by the suddenness of the attack, Little Wolf scampered into his hole like any other little wolf, and crouched in the darkness shivering with fear. Some time passed, during which he could hear the wail of the women and the victorious cries of the Otoes; then the noises ceased. With a great pang of remorse, the consciousness of his cowardice came upon Little Wolf. He had crawled into a hole like a badger!

Then he thought of Hinnagi.

He crawled out of the hole and ran down the hill into the village with his wolf skin still upon him. There amid the tepees he saw the bodies of some of the old men who had attempted resistance, but the time of their strength was passed.

"Hinnagi! Hinnagi!" called Little Wolf. He listened, and heard only the wail of the women from the lodges.

It was the custom of the Otoes to carry off the fairest daughters of the enemy as the spoil of war. Little Wolf thought of this with a great pang at his heart. A great indefinite resolve of heroism came upon him. He ran out of the village and down the valley, keeping the trail of the enemy. When he had gone some distance, he came upon some ponies that the Otoes had abandoned for the fresher ones from the herds of the Omahas.

Catching one of these, weary with a long trail, he mounted it and turned its head down the trail of the Otoes, urging its weary limbs into a gallop by plying his heels upon its ribs.

The shades of the valley crept slowly up the hills and the golden glow faded from the summits. Little Wolf still urged the stumbling pony through the darkness. As he rode, the frenzy that he had felt in the war dance rushed through him. His temples beat and his heart throbbed to the time of the snarling drums. To him the night breeze seemed heavy with noble deeds awaiting to be given life and voices of thunder for the ears of men.

He felt that in some indefinite way he would now become a strong *waschusha!* The Otoes had stolen the ponies and the women; ah, that included Hinnagi! He would save them; little did he know how, yet he felt that he would save them. Then the braves would not laugh at him any more, but would let him ride to battle with them. And maybe sometime Hinnagi would be his squaw!

Suddenly rounding the base of a hill, the pony stopped short and pricked up its ears, sniffing the wind that came up the gulch. Little Wolf, aroused from his musing, soon understood the abruptness of the pony. He smelled smoke! Slipping to the ground he crawled on his hands and knees up the gulch in the direction from which the scent of the smoke came.

Soon he reached the end of the gulch and, looking into a small valley, he saw through the gloom a number of rudely constructed tepees. Breathlessly he listened. For awhile there was no sound except the crackling of the low fires and the flap of the blankets about the poles. Then as he listened, there came to his ears a low, mournful wail as of a night wind in the scrub oaks of a bluff.

Having satisfied himself that the Otoes slept soundly, Little Wolf crawled in the direction of the wail and disappeared in the gloom.

Some moments afterward, an Otoe brave suddenly awoke from his heavy slumber. In the weird glow of the falling fire he beheld at the entrance of his tepee a grey wolf standing motionless.

The brave raised himself upon his elbow, uttering a grunt of terror as of one who feels a nightmare and would cry out were not his tongue frozen in his mouth.

The wolf with a startled movement whispered hoarse-

ly in the Omaha tongue: "The Omahas! They are coming! Fly! Fly!"

The Otoe brave leaped to his feet, every limb growing
cold with fright. He rubbed his eyes and stared at the
darkness. The wolf had vanished.

Now an Indian believes weird things, and the warning of a talking wolf was not a thing to be despised even
though it were only dreamed. So the Otoe brave gave a
shout that rang up the gulch and made the grazing ponies
snort and tug at their lariats.

Soon the entire band was rushing about the camp.

"The Omahas! They are coming!" cried the startled
brave. "Fly! Fly! For lo, a grey wolf came to my tepee
and spoke to me in a dream!"

"Fly! Fly!" echoes the whole band, delirious with fear.
"Kill the squaws!" they shouted; for in their flight they
could not be burdened with their spoils, and they would
not leave them to their enemies.

There was the sound of the shrieks of women; then
the galloping of hoofs; then silence.

Two days afterward the Omahas, having returned to
their stricken village, made the trail of the fleeing Otoes
thunderous with pursuing hoofs. Suddenly topping the
hill that overlooked the deserted camp of their enemies,
they beheld the bodies of the slain women strewn amid
the tepees. Over one of these a grey wolf stood.

There was a shout from the foremost of the Omaha
warriors, and a dozen arrows sang in the air and quivered
in the body of the wolf. It rolled upon its side with a cry
half human!

47

A group of braves, riding up to the corpse of the woman, pulled the blanket from its face.

It was Hinnagi!

With a savage kick one turned the still quivering body of the wolf upon its back. The grey hide fell from an emaciated brown face, twitching with the agony of death.

It was Little Wolf!

Overland Monthly, December 1901

The Smile of God

The Omahas were hunting bison. The young moon had been thin and bent like a bow by the arm of a strong man when they had left their village in the valley of Ne Shuga. Night after night it had grown above their cheerless tepees, ever further eastward, until now it came forth no more, but lingered in its black lodge like a brave who has walked far and keeps his blankets because the way was hard and long.

All through the time of the growing and dying moon, the Omahas had sought for the bison. Upon a hundred summits they had halted to gaze beneath the arched hand into the lonely valleys from whence came no sound of lowing cows or bellowing bulls. Like the voice of Famine through the lonesome air came the *caw-caw* of the crow. Like heaps of bleaching bones the far-off sage brush whitened.

This evening as the women busied themselves with the building of the tepees, there was no crooning on their lips. The valley in which they were placing their camp was still but for the clattering of the poles, as they were placed in their conical positions, or the flap of the blankets, which were being bound about the poles for a covering.

At dreary intervals a grazing pony would toss its weary head and neigh nervously, as if wondering at the stillness of its masters.

The silent squaws gathered armfuls of scrub oak and plum twigs, and lit fires that lapped the blackening air with ruddy tongues and sent their voices roaring up the hills, to be answered by their echoes that came back faintly like the lowing of a phantom herd!

The old men and the braves sat about the fires and no word was on their lips. From lip to lip the fragrant pipe passed, yet even its softening influence could not move to speech the lips it touched. Each face upon which the firelight fell was hideous with the gauntness of hunger.

One by one of the runners, sent out in search of the herds, came into camp. With a slow, swinging trot these great lean men approached, as the gaunt wolf approaches his lair in the cold light of the morning when no prey has been abroad all night. Sullen and silent they took their places in the cheerless circles about the fires. There was no need for words from them. Their expectant kinsmen looked into their faces and read the tale of their despair so readily from the drawn skin and sunken eyes that they groaned.

The glow of the west fell into the greyness of ashes, as a camp fire falls when all the women sleep. Then the dark came over the eastern hills. Far into the night the braves and old men sat about the fires, speechless. As they listened, they could hear the hungry children whining in

THE SMILE OF GOD

their sleep. Once a squaw, suddenly awakened from a
dream near the fires, leaped to her feet and cried "*Tae!
Tae!* [bison]" The hoarse cry beat against the black hills
and came back like a mockery. The men gazed at each
other and grinned with twitching lips.

Again the lonesome air slumbered, save for a weird
song that arose from the tepee of the big medicine-man,
Ashunhunga. He was calling to Wakunda. The song
droned itself into silence like the song of a locust when
the evening is quiet.

After some time, a sound of wailing came from the
mysterious tepee; and as the men turned their faces to the
place, they beheld the half-naked form of the medicine-
man passing like a spectre amid the glow of the fires.

The dry skin clung to his ribs and sinews. His head
was thrown back and the fires lit his face. Through his
parted lips the white teeth shone. Out of the hollows of
his eyes a wild light glared. The dream was upon him!
With bony hands clenched, he beat his naked breast and
cried: "*Wah-hoo-ha-a! Wah-hoo-ha-a-a-a!* The curse of
Wakunda is upon us! The black spirits of the dead are
about us! For Ashunhunga had a dream. A black spirit
came to him and its eyes were lightning and its voice
was thunder as it said: 'Why do you shelter him whom
Wakunda hates?' *Wa-hoo-ha-a-a-a!*"

Blood fell from the mysterious man's palms where the
nails clenched convulsively, and his arms and breast were
smeared with blood. The listeners shuddered as the wild
voice began anew.

"Ashunhunga will talk to the black spirit! He will

learn whom Wakunda hates! Him we shall cast from us! Then Wakunda will smile and the valleys shall thunder with herds!"

Beating his breast and gesticulating wildly with his long, bony arms, the old man passed back amid the tepees.

Those who sat about the fires were frozen by the wild words into bronze statues of Fear. Scarcely was a breath drawn; not a man moved. The black spirits of the dead were about them! Not a hand was raised to replenish the fires with faggots. The flames sank, and the embers sent a dull blue light upon the circles of haggard faces!

As Ashunhunga passed on toward his tepee, he suddenly stumbled over a shivering form, huddled in the shadow. Quickly regaining his feet, he saw that upon which he had stumbled. It was a dwarfed, ill-shapen body, with short, crooked legs and long emaciated arms with protruding joints. The form raised itself upon its hands and knees and looked upon the medicine-man with an idiot leer upon its face.

It was Shanugahi (Nettle) the cripple.

With a cry as of a squaw who sees a black spirit in her sleep, Ashunhunga rushed into his tepee. His mystical songs wailed over the camp for a while, then ceased. Overcome by his fanatical emotions, he had fallen into a swoon. And he had a dream.

He was alone upon the prairie and hunger was pinching his entrails. Then there came a bison bull toward him, roaring through the silence. He raised his bow, and with sure aim, sent an arrow singing into the heart of the beast. Then the air grew black, save for a blue light as of dying fires. The bison began to change form! Its hind legs grew short and crooked; its fore legs became long and lean and sinewy like the arms of a starving man. Its body dwindled, dwindled—and it was human! Its head became indistinct and wavered as in a haze. Then it grew boldly up in the ghastly light and the face was the face of Shanugahi with the idiot leer!

The vision whirled giddily and sank into the dizzy darkness.

With a cry as of one stabbed in his sleep, Ashunhunga sprang from his blanket and rushed out of his tepee. Those who sat about the smouldering fires, startled from their dumb terror by the cry, raised their eyes and gazed upon the face of the medicine-man as he passed. They did not speak, but the question on their faces was "who?"

"It is Shanugahi!" said Ashunhunga in an awing whisper. "It is Shanugahi whom Wakunda hates! He has brought the curse upon us!"

The ill-shapen bronze mass of flesh that was Shanugahi lay curled up in sleep in the shadow of a tepee. Suddenly his sleep was broken by a heavy hand reaching out of the darkness. He shook himself, raised his head and gazed about. He saw the faces of a number of braves indistinct in the dim glow of the fires. Nearby a pony stood ready for a rider. Then a strange voice close to his ear, whispered hoarsely: "Fly! Fly! The black spirits of the dead are about you! The curse of Wakunda is upon you! Fly! Fly!"

Shanugahi stared about him, then turned his meaningless eyes upon his tribesmen and leered. Strong arms seized him and placed him astride the waiting pony. Someone lashed the animal across the haunches, and it plunged down the valley into the blackness of the night.

When the dazed rider had gone some distance, the meaning of the whispered words came upon him. Cold sweat sprang out on his limbs. He glanced about him, and the night was swarming with demons!

His shriek cut the stillness like a knife of ice! He grasped the mane of the pony with a convulsive clasp. He dashed his heels into the flanks of the terrified brute! The lone gulches thundered with the beat of hoofs. Bushes flew past, and each was a pursuing black spirit!

Shanugahi clung closely to the pony's back, hiding his face in its tossing mane, clasping its neck with the strength of madness, pressing its ribs with his knees until the straining animal groaned with pain and fright. Through valleys, over hills, down gulches they fled! Clumps of sage brush flitted past, and each was a heap of whitened bones!

It was like falling in a nightmare through an immeasurable black pit, save for the scamper of the coyote as it sought the gulches, whining, or the tumbling flight of the owl or bat, fleeing with wings that whirred in the stillness!

The pace of the pony became slower and slower. Its breath came in short, rasping gasps. Then with a last effort of its terrified limbs, it took the long incline of a high hill, and upon the bare summit tumbled to its knees. Shanugahi rolled off its back, and horse and rider, worn out, swooned upon the summit.

When Shanugahi awoke, the pale light that foregoes the coming sun lay upon the shivering hills. He looked about him and saw a circle of grey wolves staring at him with eyes like small moons dawn-stricken. He felt about him for a weapon, but found only his stone pipe and a pouch of red willow bark.

He filled his pipe and striking a spark from a bit of flint that strewed the summit, he lit it. Then the sun peeped over the far sky line and with its horizontal rays touched the hills with fire. Its light warmed the frozen nerves of Shanugahi. He puffed grey rings of smoke into the air.

At length, taking his pipe from his mouth, he reared his hideous body in the glow of the morning, and with a long, bony arm, raised his pipe to the smiling sun in silent invocation. For some time, motionless, he stood like a being of the black depths praying for mercy from the shining heights. Then he uttered two words.

"*Wakunda! Tae!*" (O God! Bison!)

The staring wolves, moved by the wild voice, raised their noses to the heavens with a howl, and slunk away into the gulches. The sun rose higher and higher, and Shanugahi breathed into his veins the laughing gold of the morning. With all the simplicity of his nature, he forgot the terror of the night. It was to him as some vague dream, dreamed many summers past. Yet the one fixed idea of finding the bison swayed his whole being.

His hunger had reached that stage in which it acts like

a heavy draught of some subtle intoxicant. The stupor of days past had been changed into a joyous and even hopeful delirium. And as he looked upon the sun, to him it was the smile of Wakunda! Now he would find the bison.

He caught his pony, grazing near by, and leaping upon its back, urged its stiffened limbs into a jog and took the lonesome stretch of prairie with song upon his lips. All day the pony jogged across the prairie at an easy pace toward the west. At that time of the evening when the coolness comes with the dew, and the bugs awake with drowsy hummings among the grasses, Shanugahi caught a roaring sound as of some sullen storm that thunders beneath the horizon.

He checked his pony and placing his hands to his ears, listened intently. He knew the sound! Dismounting, he crawled to the top of a hill and gazed into a broad valley.

As far as he could see, straining his eyes, the valley was black with bison! For a moment he stood spellbound; then a great joy lashed his blood into a frenzy. He rushed to his pony and mounting, turned its head to the east. The night came down, and still Shanugahi held his pony to a fast gallop. His brain whirled giddily. Now he had found the bison! His people would not starve. He sang and shouted and laughed until his voice broke into a cackle! The delirium of the rider was caught by the pony. With all the might of long generations of prairie herds, it sent the thundering hills and valleys under its feet.

At that time of the morning when the east grows pale, and sleep is the deepest, the famished tribe, having moved a weary day's journey westward, was sleeping heavily. Suddenly a hoarse shout shattered their dreams and made the hills clamorous with echoes!

The whole camp leaped from its blankets and stared with blinking eyes in the direction of the shout.

There, upon the brow of a hill that overlooked the camp, stood a horse and rider set in bold relief against the pale sky of morning. With a long, bony arm the rider pointed to the westward and again he cried in a weak, broken voice:

"*Tae! Tae!*" (Bison! bison!)

Then horse and rider collapsed like the figures of a dream that wavers with the morning. A number of men rushing up the hill, found the bodies of the pony and Shanugahi. Upon the lips of the dead rider lingered a calm smile as of contentment.

"It is the smile of Wakunda," said one old man in awe.

"Wakunda smiles! Wakunda smiles!" shouted the men. The whole camp caught up the cry. "Bison! Bison! Wakunda smiles!"

And when the sun arose, they were moving westward on the trail of Shanugahi.

Two nights afterward there was joy in the camp of the Omahas. Having found the long-sought-for herd, they had feasted heavily, and now they slept as the wolf sleeps when the prey has not escaped. Beside a fire two old men were still awake, and as they smoked, they talked of Shanugahi. He had found the herd. Wakunda had smiled upon him; and yet Shanugahi was ugly and a cripple!

"Ugh!" they both grunted after a thoughtful silence, shaking their heads in wonderment at so incomprehensible a thing.

Then they wrapped themselves in their blankets, and slept.

Overland Monthly, January 1902

The Fading
of Shadow Flower

She was only a timid little Omaha maiden with a pair
of pensive eyes, dark like the thunder clouds, and like
them, fraught with a potential fire that seemed ever
about to spend its fury in the weakness of tears. She
passed her childhood hours beside the singing streams
and in the lonesome places where the silence lingered.
The sunrise and the sunset found her where the wild
flowers clustered, or where the noises of the nesting
birds disturbed the stillness of the thickets. For hers was
a timorous soul, and the dumb kindness of the green
things was sweet to her.

So, as she grew in this wise toward the mysterious
time when the immaturity of the girl bursts into the
magic of the woman, her people said: "She talks with the
things that talk not; she plays with the wind that sleeps
and moans in the shadowy place." And that is why they
named her Shadow Flower.

In the long, mysterious nights of the winter, Shadow
Flower wept with fear at the mournful cry of the coyotes, and often through the droning days of the summer
did the harsh warning of the startled rattlesnake send her

trembling in terror to her mother's breast. Yet, huddled close to the group about the evening fire, she loved to listen to the warriors' tale of the strong arm and the fierce heart; and her eyes glowed with an unwonted light as her kinsmen recounted the wild swoop of the ambushed foe or the silent pursuit, swift and relentless.

All the glowing ideals of manly prowess that her maiden heart had conjured, were centered in the person of the fearless brave, Big Axe; for had he not the eagle glance that went to the heart of an enemy like an arrow? Was not his the shaggy head of the buffalo bull that strikes with fear the boldest hunter? The breath of his sinewy breast was like a whirlwind when the battle cry awakened in his throat! There was no arm in all the circled tepees that could hurl a tomahawk so straight and far; and none that could heave above the anger of the battle a war club more ponderous!

"Ah," she would say to herself, while wandering alone with her musings, "Big Axe is so great a man!"

When a band of warriors rode out of the village, bent upon some petty conquest somewhere beyond the blue hills that undulated the horizon with their summits, Shadow Flower would become very lonely, and she would stand for long hours upon some larger hill, scanning the dim sky line for the returning warriors; for where the battle was, there was Big Axe. And when at last she would catch sight of the returning band, shouting with the great joy of a battle won, how proudly she stared, and with what a light in her eyes, at her graceful warrior astride his swift pony! How anxiously would she search the headdress of her brave for the fresh eagle feather that should speak of some late deed done by the strong arm—her strong arm!

Yet her timorous little soul alone knew of the great overflowing passion that she treasured for Big Axe; unless, perhaps, the birds and the green things understood her, for hers was a passion that little words could not carry.

Thus did the frail flower long for the golden kisses of the sun!

There was war between the Omaha and Ponca tribes. So it happened one morning, in the time when the deer tear the earth with their horns, that Shadow Flower, hunting late blossoms upon the sere hills where the young Dawn danced, heard below her the impatient stamp of ponies, and beheld the mounting of braves, for Big Axe was leading a party of a hundred warriors against the enemy.

The purple spikes of the ironweed and the yellow plumes of the golden-rod dropped from her fingers as she gazed upon the sight below her. What a sight! It was as the marshalling of the incarnate Winds from the circle of the heavens. Out of the dust cloud that arose from the dry earth where four hundred nervous hoofs fretted with impatience beneath the restraining thongs, she caught the dazzle of the sleek and vari-coloured hides of the ponies; some white with the brilliance of the summer sun when it glares upon the false lakes of alkali; some spotted and wiry as the wild cat; some tawny as the mountain lion; some black like the midnight when the storm clouds fly.

Their gaunt flanks were heaving with the joy of speed and power. Their nostrils were distent with the influx of prairie winds that know no restraining hand save that of the great invisible Master. They snorted and reared as if about to plunge in a wild heat down the winds. Their neighing was the shout of the tempest in the rocks, and their gusty manes were as clouds that tatter in the storm.

And amid this *mêlée* of dust and noise and dazzle trembled the gaudy headdresses of the warriors, bright with the painted wing feathers of the eagle and the hawk.

Now a shout drowns the neighing and the snorting. A hundred braves leap to the backs of the plunging ponies. The dust cloud thickens and sweeps down the valley like a whirlwind. A far glint of brandished weapons; a dying shout; the band swoops about the base of a hill. Then the sultry day drones and drowses on the prairie. The grasshopper breaks the slumber of the stillness with his snapping noise; a lone hawk skirts the ground with slow, circling flight. But Shadow Flower stands and stares beneath a shading hand into the brilliance where the warriors vanished. Her ears hear not the snarl and hum of the drowsy bugs, nor the shrill chatter of the sly gopher as it rears its striped body from the grass and peers about. She sees not the circling hawk and scarcely does the glitter of the yellow grass hurt her eyes. For her ears are filled with the shout that has died, and in her eyes a sinewy, masterful brave urges a black pony down the valley.

After a while her hand dropped from her eyes, and catching sight of the circling hawk, she cried: "O you who are so keen of eye, tell me, can you not see into the heart of Muzape Tunga [Big Axe]? O you who are so keen of thought, tell me, does he think of Pazha Hu [Shadow Flower]?"

But the hawk circled far away and the day droned on.

Among the hills, hidden from one who looked and saw not, the war party rode on with the noses of its ponies to that portion of the sky from which the red sun of summer springs, for in that direction lay the village of the Poncas, perched upon the yellow bluffs of the great muddy river.

On the evening of the second day the air grew soft with the scent of flowing waters, and the Omahas, checking their ponies upon the brow of a hill, beheld to their right the swirling stream, red with the last light of the day; and before them, across a deep hollow, the village of the Poncas, upon the summit of a bluff.

But while their eyes wandered over the misty stretches of the river, a wild shout startled the calm of the scene, while from the village on the opposite summit a line of mounted warriors issued, taking the precipitous hillside at a brisk gallop.

The sudden shout and the beat of flying hoofs hurled the weary ponies of the Omahas back upon their haunches. Yet scarcely had the echoes of the shout cried their last among the distant bluffs, when a hundred Omaha bow thongs twanged and a hundred arrows shrieked their shrill death-song in the quiet evening air. A second and a third flight of arrows, and the rushing Poncas were thrown into confusion. Those in the rear were thrown by the floundering bodies of the wounded ponies in the front, the fury of their momentum hurling them pellmell into the valley below. Then the Omahas swept down the valley, as the eagle sweeps, with the battle cry upon their lips, and the remnant of the attacking Poncas turned and fled up the steep hillside to their village.

The village of the Poncas, in addition to its strong position, was further fortified by stockades, constructed of saplings driven into the ground with their tops sharpened. The fugitives having gained the protection of this barrier, were safe from further pursuit, and emboldened by their protection, they hurled such a flight of arrows into the ranks of the enraged Omahas that the latter were obliged to withdraw beyond arrow flight, contenting themselves with taunting their besieged foes by displaying the dripping scalps of the fallen.

Now the influence of the fading evening cooled the anger and hushed the shouting. From the height whither the assaulting band withdrew to camp, one could hurl the triumphant gaze unnumbered bowshots westward, athwart the brown hills that seemed to have been stricken motionless in liquid turbulence by the enchantment of the sunset, marvellous with the pomp of streamers, violet, purple, saffron, sanguine, dun!

Far up the river the blue haze of the sky-fringed woodland blended into the purple shadow beneath the contrasting yellow of the bluffs, that looked down into the smooth waters, upon their own scarred and wrinkled images crowned with golden crowns by the last scant sunlight. The cottonwoods placed their long shadows like soothing fingers on the muddy madness of the central stream. The Night awakened in the east and stretched its long black arms into the west, and the glory vanished. The distant woodland and the bluffs grew into indistinguishable masses. The river became a faint film above a lower concave of dawning stars. The camp fires in the village reared long towers of light into the darkness, then fell back into a sleepy glow.

One dreaming out a sunset on the prairie cannot wonder at the exquisite hyperbole of the Omaha language; that tongue nurtured amid marvelous possibilities of fury and calm, of beauty and terror, all within the sight-tiring circle of stupendous distance.

The dawn came, and by the first light the Poncas beheld their enemies camped across the valley. Upon one side the bluff fell sheer to the river; upon the other lingered a cruel and patient foe. So it happened that after many days, moans of suffering arose from the lodges on the bluff; and the Omahas laughed in their tepees, for the sound of an enemy's wailing is sweet. The sweltering suns of the prairie September beat upon the bare summit where the village pined, and the lips of the Poncas burned with thirst, while their eyes drank of the copious floods far below them.

So it chanced one day, when a cry went up through the village: "Our children are dying of thirst; let us beg mercy of our enemies!" that an unarmed brave passed out of the village and across the valley toward the camp of his foes. With tottering step he approached the tepee before which Big Axe waited. His lips were swollen and cracked; his eyes were bleared and sunken, yet they glared as the eyes of a wolf from the darkness of a cavern.

In a hoarse, inarticulate whisper he spoke to the chief: "Pity my people, for they are dying of thirst!"

There was lightning in the eyes of Muzape Tunga. "Badger!" he hissed; and he struck the suppliant down before him.

The sun burned down the glaring blue of the west. A continuous wail arose from the suffering village like the cry of pines in a gentle wind; while from the tepees of the besiegers came the sound of merry laughter that mocked like the babble of inaccessible waters.

But when the red sun touched the tops of the far hills, another form left the enclosure of the village and took its way down the hillside. As it came nearer, a hush of awe fell upon the Omahas. The form was that of a squaw! With an unfaltering movement she approached, seeming to hover through the mist that arose from the valley. Slowly she climbed the hillside. Not a sound passed the lips of the beholders. They seemed the figures of one dream gazing at the central idea of another. The form emerged from the mist and stood, swathed in the chromatic radiance of the evening before the motionless figure of Muzape Tunga. The eyes of the woman and the chief met in unwavering stare. Had the glance of the former become vocal, it would have been a song with the softness of the mother's lullaby, but with a meaning terrible as the battle cry of a brave.

With a langorous movement the woman raised her

arms, thus allowing the many-coloured skin that hung about her shoulders to slip to the ground, exposing all the dumb eloquence of her brown breasts. Out of the silence her voice broke like the voice of a sudden wind that rises in the night.

"Nunda Nu [Man-Heart] fears not Muzape Tunga!"

The chief saw the lithe young form, heard the soft, caressing voice and shivered with great passion.

A swift smile crossed the face of the young woman, soft as a last ray of sunlight on a hill. Again the voice grew out of the hush.

"The heart of Muzape Tunga is strong like his arm and kind like his eye; he will spare my people."

The chief's great breast heaved with the pleasure of his eye and ear. "Nunda Nu has the heart of a man and the eye of a woman," he said; "her voice is soft like the song of a forest stream; Muzape Tunga spares her people."

Nunda Nu turned her face to her village and made a signal with her uplifted hands. Soon an unarmed Ponca, manifestly a chief by his garments, was seen taking his way down the hillside.

"Come!" said Nunda Nu, turning to Big Axe; "my father bears the pipe of peace; let us meet him in the valley."

Without a word the chief followed the young woman, while his warriors stared after in wonderment. In the valley, midway between the village and the camp, the chiefs met. Then both sitting cross-legged upon the grass, the Ponca lit the pipe of peace, and having puffed silently for a while, handed it to his conqueror. The sweet smoke of the red willow arose slowly over the silent three, and Big Axe stared abstractedly into the mounting vapour. The evening grew old. The sunlight left the summits of the hills and the shadows deepened. Still Big Axe did not speak, but gazed with wide eyes into the ascending cloud of smoke. The heart of the terrible warrior had grown tender; a light softer than the twilight was in his eye. It seemed that he could hear the slumberous, singing voice of a squaw and the prattle of children about the door of his lodge. There were pictures for him in the rising smoke.

Suddenly he took the pipe from his mouth and returned it to the Ponca chief.

"We will bury the tomahawk," he said; "our ponies shall sweat no more in the battle, but in the paths of the bison. No more shall our faces be cruel with warpaint."

Again there was silence but for the rhythmic puffing of the Ponca's pipe. Again Muzape Tunga spoke, and his voice was sonorous with passion.

"The eyes of Nunda Nu are deep and dark as a mountain lake; her voice is a song that the slow winds sing in the willows. Give me Nunda Nu that my lodge may be filled with laughter; give her to Muzape Tunga that peace may be everlasting between us!"

There was a silence. The Ponca forgot his pipe; he puffed deliberately and at long intervals. The ascending smoke dwindled to a thin grey thread. With steadfast gaze the smoker looked before him into the darkness, for his thoughts were deep.

At length he laid the pipe upon the grass and arose to

his feet, extending his hand to Big Axe. His voice was tremulous as he spoke.

"Muzape Tunga asks a great thing of his conquered brother; had he asked for a hundred ponies, with feet fleet as the winds in winter, his brother would have laughed at the little gift. Nunda Nu is my life; I give my life to my brother."

Already the night had spread into the west and the darkness hid their parting.

Some days afterward at sunset, an Omaha maiden stood upon a hill near her village. With hand at brow she peered into the blue distance. Suddenly a cry of delight trembled on her lips. A cloud of dust had grown far away upon the verge of a hill to the northeast, slowly resolving itself into a long line of warriors approaching at a gallop. The column drew nearer. The face of the watching maiden grew darker with anxiety, as a brilliant cloud darkens when the twilight fails. She beheld the masterful form of Big Axe mounted upon a black pony, riding in advance of the band; yet her face darkened. Her brows lowered with the strain of her intense gaze. Was it a squaw that rode upon a pony white as a summer cloud beside her warrior?

A shout went up from the village below. The speed of the ponies was increased to a fast gallop; the band swept up the valley. A strange low cry fell from the lips of the maiden; a stifled cry like that of a sleeping brave who feels the knife of the treacherous foeman at his heart.

In the village was the sound of many glad voices; but

in the darkness of the hill above, a frail form buried its face in the dry bunch grass and uttered a moan that no one heard.

The autumn passed: the cold winds came down from the north, shaking the snow from their black wings, and the people of the village began to look upon Shadow Flower with awe. For never a word had she spoken to anyone since the returning of the band in the fall. With a dull light in her eyes she wandered about muttering to herself: "It was summer when they left; now the prairie is so cold and white, so cold and white."

Absent-mindedly she would dwell upon the bitter words, gazing beneath an arched hand into the cold, white glare of the horizon. Then her eyes, at times, would blaze with gladness. "Shonga saba! Shonga saba!" (a black pony) she would cry ecstatically; and for one intense moment her frail form would be erect and quivering with joy. Then the light in her eye would fade as the fires fade in a camp that is deserted; a cry of anguish would fall from her lips, her hand would drop lifelessly from her brow. "No," she would sigh languidly; "no, it is only a cloud! O, the prairie is so cold and white, so cold and white!"

And the old people shook their heads and whispered to each other: "The soul of Pazha Hu has followed the summer, for her soul loved the flowers; can you not hear her body crying for her soul?"

When the warm winds came again and the hills were green, the crying of a young child was heard in the lodge

70

of Muzape Tunga. The simple heart of the stern warrior throbbed with gladness as a cold seed throbs with the blowing of the south wind.

But the sound of the infant's voice brought no summer to the heart of Nunda Nu. The touch of its little brown hands stung her breasts, and as she looked upon its face, placid or expressive as its dreams took form or slept, a cold shudder ran through her veins as when one gazes on a snake, for it was the child of an enemy.

All through the long winter a slow hate had sapped the kindness from the heart of the future mother; and when she felt the new life throbbing into form, her thoughts grew bitter. So now the unforgotten moaning of the children of her people, dying with thirst upon the barren summit, was loud enough to drown the prattle of her enemy's child, which should have wrought enchantment in her blood.

One night a noiseless shadow passed among the tepees hushed in slumber beneath the moonlight. It crept up to the tepee of Muzape Tunga and crouched beside it in an attitude of listening. The bugs chirped and hummed, the frogs croaked, the wolves howled far away; save these and a sleeper's heavy breathing, there was silence.

Suddenly there was a faint sound as of someone moving in the tepee; the shadow outside arose and the moonlight fell upon its haggard face, the face of Shadow Flower. She placed her eye to a small opening in the skins that covered the poles. Now she would gaze upon the child of Muzape Tunga!

Through the opening at the top of the tepee the moonlight entered with intense brilliance and fell upon three faces. One was the face of her once sweet dream and the face that trembled through the visions of her madness, Muzape Tunga's. One was the beautiful, cruel face of her who came upon a pony white as a summer cloud that autumn evening when the sunlight left the prairie. One was a face that she had not seen before, yet her poor heart ached as she looked upon it. It was the face of his child, her child. Ah, it should have been the child of Shadow Flower, she thought, and her brain reeled with sudden madness.

As she looked, the woman in the tepee raised herself upon her elbow. She gazed upon the peaceful face of Big Axe. The moon lit up her features in clear relief. Her eyes were terrible with hate; the lids drawn closely about them until they had the small beady appearance of the snake's. Her lips were drawn closely cross her white teeth in a cold grin. Her form trembled as with a chill, yet the night was warm. Then she arose, and with a noiseless step, sought for something that hung upon the side of the tepee. She returned clutching a tomahawk. The light caught her whole form, making it stand out, clear-cut like a statue, the statue of a prairie Judith.

Then she bent over the sleeping Muzape Tunga for one moment. There was a dull sound as the weapon entered the sleeper's skull; but more than this there was no sound, no groan. And the one who stood like a shadow without the tepee was stricken dumb with fright.

The woman within turned to the sleeping child and

raised the dripping tomahawk; but her arm seemed to freeze in act to strike, and the blow did not fall. A strange soft light crept over the face of the woman. She lowered her arm and laid the weapon aside. Then with the step of a wild-cat she crept to the entrance of the tepee and, gazing cautiously about for a moment, slipped silently into the haze of the moonlight, and was engulfed in the darkness of the valley.

As the dim outline of the fleeing squaw mixed itself with the uncertain haze and vanished, a great happiness leaped into the stagnant veins of Shadow Flower, and her blood rushed like a stream when the ice melts with the breath of the south wind.

Even the thought that Big Axe lay dead within the tepee did not quell her happiness, for she said to herself: "Now Pazha Hu shall have her warrior; he shall be all hers."

She crept into the tepee and, kneeling, put her lips to the chilling lips of Big Axe. He did not breathe. She placed her arms about his body, her face against his breast, yet he did not move. He lay quietly with the intense moonlight upon his face. She did not sob, she was almost happy; for did she not at last possess that for which she had pined?

Her musings were broken by the crying of the child. She took it in her arms and held it to her breast, humming a low lullaby, half-persuaded that the child was her own. But the child was frightened by the strange voice and cried piteously. Then Shadow Flower thought, "It cries for its father, yet its father has gone." "Hush!" she said to the child; "we will go and find the soul of Muzape Tunga; it cannot be far away."

She wrapped a blanket about the infant, muffling its cries, and tied it about her shoulders. Then she went silently through the village and out into the open prairie, weird with the blue haze of the moon and the lonesome cries of the wolves.

A rabbit hopped past and stopped near her as if gazing at the maiden.

"O Rabbit!" cried Shadow Flower, "tell me, have you seen the soul of Muzape Tunga?"

The rabbit, awed by the strangeness of the voice, moved its long ears; then it hopped away into the shades. The maiden followed and was swallowed in the moonlit mist.

When the sun looked into the village, the women were stricken with terror and the men with anger. The wise people shook their heads by which to say: "Ah, yes; we thought such things of Nunda Nu."

The days passed; the moons came and went; yet Shadow Flower did not return. There was a common thought concerning her disappearance which was never spoken aloud; but when the fires burned low and the night grew late, it was often whispered with awe:

"She has gone in search of her soul; it fled last year with the summer."

Overland Monthly, February 1903

A Prairie Borgia

Wazhinga Saba was a great Medicine Man. An old Indian whose original being has not been blasted by the doubt of the white man, will tell you that he was a seer of strange things big in meaning; a dreamer of dreams that glared with the light of dawns and days, sundowns and stars, speaking with the ambiguous tongue of mystery! To his credulous subjects, Wazinga Saba was a bronze Colossus, stretching a hard metallic hand across his little world, and the little world groaned or laughed according to the will of the many-mooded master; for such have been the people since the creation, and such have been the masters.

In the fall of the year 1812 the entire Omaha tribe, returning from a buffalo hunt on the plains which now constitute Western Nebraska, built its winter village at a distance of about 200 miles from Ne Shuga, the Great River.

The hunting had been poor, and the tribe, though originally intending to winter among the protecting bluffs of the great stream, where firewood was plentiful, discontinued its march in order to conserve its strength.

Who toils must eat much; therefore the tribe ceased toiling that the small stock of meat might endure the winter.

The Omahas built comfortable mud lodges along the banks of a creek, which would at once afford clean water and a limited supply of wood from the scattered plum thickets.

The fall days passed and the Northwest breathed with snowy breath upon the hills, and the tribe was locked in the desolate little valley as by a hand of ice. Confinement to the lodges and insufficiency of food brought sickness. Many a strong brave became less than the shadow of a squaw. Many a squaw tottered and fell beneath her load, and became weaker than the child at her back.

It was one of the numerous humble tragedies that history does not see.

But daily about the windswept village went a youth who entered the lodges where the groans of suffering were loudest. There was a strange light in his eye, and he who from the bed of sickness saw the light trusted in the youth and muttered to his kinsmen: "Did you not see the light in the eye of this youth? Wakunda smiles upon him—his power is great!"

This the people did not guess. The light was the glare of the life that was being consumed within him, blown upon by the strong breath of the winter and the hunger. For wherever the youth went he brought not only the mysterious drinks brewed from herbs, but he brought morsels of meat which he himself should have eaten.

And it happened that some of the stricken died and the greater part lived. Then a small noise of voices with a big meaning spread throughout the village. A buzz of wonder, which was full of the doings of the youth, whom the people learned to call Wazadi (Healer).

In all races have appeared these sacrificing men of genius. Some have been Christs in their small way; some have remained unappreciated martyrs. All have contributed to the upbuilding of belief in the supernatural. These are the incarnations of Pity, grotesque in a world of cruelty and suffering. Many have missed immortality but by the length of Pilate's judgment.

The noise of wondering voices spread and swelled into a cry that beat into the lodge of the stern and selfish chief, Wazhinga Saba. And as he heard, the little warmth that hid in his heart died and the coldness came; for jealousy is the northwest wind of the soul.

Many days he sat alone in his lodge, speaking only with the jealousy of his heart. He said to himself: "Am I not the greatest of all medicine men? Shall a youth walk between Wazhinga Saba and the belief of his people?"

Then the coldness of his heart answered things that would have been terrible upon a tongue. And the Chief listened.

So it happened one evening that a runner came to the lodge of the youth called Wazadi, summoning him to go to the big chief's lodge. Wazadi followed the runner to the big lodge.

He pushed aside the buffalo hide that hung across the door and entered. The chief, dressed in his most elaborate garments, profusely decorated with wolfs' teeth and hawks' beaks, sat alone by his fire. As the youth entered, the chief arose and stood in the glare of the flames that gave an additional attraction to his regal figure. For a moment Wazadi stood awed into immobility at the sight, nor moved until Wazhinga Saba smiled a pleasant smile. The smile had its meaning. The Chief had wished to dazzle the youth, and it was accomplished.

Wazhinga Saba motioned the youth to sit upon the opposite side of the fire. After a prolonged silence, during which each regarded the other through the haze of flamelit smoke, the Chief said:

"The great heart of Wazhinga Saba is glad of the good words that have been spoken among the lodges. Does not the Chief love his people? The little words of a chief are big. Wazhinga Saba wishes to do great honor to Wazadi." At the name, the speaker paused and smiled again. "This place is not good," he continued; "there is an evil spirit in this place. There is much sickness and groaning and dying. It must not be. Does not the Great Chief love his people? We will take the sunrise trail; we will leave the groaning and the sickness behind us. We will go to the banks of the great smoky water. It is a good place; there are good spirits there."

The Chief paused and looked into the flames, thinking deeply. "I have a deed for a strong and brave man. A good trail must be found that the tribe may not go astray. Is Wazadi strong? Is he brave? Then let him seek a good trail to the great smoky water. Let him go alone, that the honor may not be divided like a big bison by many that are hungry!"

As Wazhinga Saba ceased speaking, a great joy born of

vanity blazed in the blood of the youth, and he answered the question in the chief's eyes with a glad voice.

"I am strong and brave! I will seek the trail!"

When Wazadi withdrew from the lodge, Wazhinga Saba sat a long time staring into the flame. He was thinking. The future was again pleasant to look upon. Ever since the noise of the strange youth's deeds had beat into the lodge, striking discord in the song that his vain heart sang, the future had been as the horizon of the morning when a black cloud blinds the eyes of the climbing sun. But now the cloud had become but a thin, translucent vapor, promising to vanish in the glare of day.

As he gazed into the fire he was thinking of the long and cruel trail which his rival would follow; of the keen and merciless storm winds, mad with the zigzag flight of snow! His reverie grew deeper. In his mind he followed the youth down the sunrise trail. He saw him wallowing through drifts, tumbling into hidden ravines; stumbling on through the blinding, hissing snow that obliterated all landmarks! He saw the white ghost of a man thrown down with hunger and the cold, to be the senseless impediment upon which the snow caught and drifted.

The last thought came like the first far cry of an approaching triumph. The Chief leaped to his feet with a loud burst of laughter. "Wazadi will not come back!" he muttered slowly as though to taste the sweetness of the words: "Wazadi will not come back! Wazadi!"

At the last word he chuckled with derision, and then lay down beside his fire. But he did not sleep. Defeat can sleep, because there is an element of death in it. Triumph is wakeful, because it is life new-born.

Before the sunrise of the next day Wazadi had disappeared among the frozen hills to the eastward. Upon the lips of Wazhinga Saba sat a smile beside a sneer. He had vanquished his budding rival and his heart held high festival.

For many days he feasted the other chiefs of the tribe, who had become puppets in his hands. Haunches of the best bison meat were wasted, until starvation stood between the tribe and the spring. And the people looked with wistful eyes upon the doings of their chief and muttered syllables of discontent like the sound of underground waters, for they dared not speak aloud.

But one evening, after many days of storm had swept across the sky, the figure of a man, frost-whitened, weakened, and blinded with the snow, stumbled into the village.

"Wazadi has come back! Wazadi has come back!"

The shout passed contagiously from lip to lip, and grew into a clamor that found its way through the door of the lodge of Wazhinga Saba. The cry wrought a terrible anger in his heart.

What! Was this the way the great Wazhinga Saba took revenge? No! He would see the blood of this audacious Wazadi! Yet it could not be done with violence, for did not the people love the youth? An oppressed people is like a pack of wolves. Both flee until the trail ends, then they turn and their bites are terrible! Would not the violent death of Wazadi end the trail?

At this thought the revenge of Wazhinga Saba became indefinite; yet some time it would be. He would wait.

These turbulent thoughts were interrupted by the entrance of the youth himself. He stood at the door of the lodge, the white ghost of a man. His eyes were sunken and bleared. The skin was drawn across his cheek bones. He tottered. His voice was the ghost of a strong voice:

"I have found the trail; the tribe will not go astray. The trail is long and there is death upon it. The winds strike like the forefeet of a bear and bite like the teeth of a wolf. I was strong and I am here. It is a bad thing for the people to take the trail!"

Wazhinga Saba smiled and answered: "Does the strong man make his toil worthless with his groaning? Wazhinga Saba speaks with the spirits. Wakunda (God) will put his hand upon the winds and they will sleep; his hand upon their teeth and they will be dull. The tribe will take the trail."

The words of the Chief flew through the village, and in their wake a groan followed. "If we take the trail we die!" muttered the people among themselves; yet the work of preparing for the march began and progressed rapidly. The little word of a chief is big; and the people feared Wazhinga Saba.

To one who has some acquaintance with the prairie, the insanity of moving an entire tribe, with its sickness and hunger, a distance of 200 miles in the dead of winter, is apparent. On the prairie there is treachery in the bluest winter sky. The Southwind that whines so abjectly in the morning, at noon may be crowned with a crown of ice in the silent North, and return a terrible Conqueror in the evening. The elemental Lackey becomes the elemental Emperor.

Wazhinga Saba, feeling that his rival was the product of the people's praise, wished to retaliate upon the people. He knew the consequences of such a movement in the winter, but the idea pleased him. He would make the tribe suffer. It would feel his power.

Throughout the village was the activity of an imminent departure. Drags were being fashioned, and upon these was packed the baggage of the tribe. There was no song among the toilers; but everywhere there was muttering and much hopeless shaking of the head. The people thought of the long trail and shivered.

One morning when the work was finished, through the pale and shivering light of the early dawn, the tribe filed out of its desolate village, and at its head walked Wazadi breaking the trail.

The sick, the old, and the children were packed like baggage on the drags. In order that the trail might be easier for those who followed, the tribe proceeded in single file, those who had extra ponies riding, and those who had none walking. So long was the column that the foremost were lost from sight among the hills when the last left the village.

By midday a heavy fall of snow began. For three days and nights the snow came, soft and gentle as a kiss that goes before betrayal. Then during the fourth night the Northwest shouted and shook the people from their shivering sleep. It was the battle cry that could not be answered.

The poles of the hastily constructed tepees groaned with the blows of the storm; many were thrown to the ground, while the blankets that were wrapped about them flapped, tore and went with the wind. The light snow scurried along the ground with a hiss like the warning of a snake, caught the madness of the storm, leaped into the air, writhing, striking, biting!

It is easy to imagine the many elemental phenomena as being merely magnifications of human passions projected upon the universe. A cyclone is sudden anger; a southwind is feminine tenderness; a rainfall is grief; the spring sunshine is love. Madness is a conglomeration of all passions. A blizzard is the madness of the air! It has the fury and blindness of anger, the hiss of hate, the shout of joy, the dusk of melancholy, the shiver of fear, the coldness of jealousy; and when its force is spent, it folds its victims in a shroud of white, which may be the act of love—a savage love!

A blizzard transforms. What it touches it leaves grotesque. It annihilates the boundary line of light and darkness. In its breath the night becomes merely a deepening of shadow upon the dim twilight of the day.

God wished to demonstrate to mankind the awful tragedy of unbridled passions, and his precept was the blizzard!

A strange, one-sided battle had begun. The Omahas, who would have turned their faces to an onslaught of the

Sioux, huddled together with their backs to the storm like a herd of lost sheep surrounded by the howl of wolves. The bravest whimpered as they blew upon their stiffened fingers. In those rare places where some one had contrived to coax a sickly fire with scant fuel, there was a jostling, fighting, crying mass of men, women and children struggling toward the glow that fought a losing fight with the breath of the storm!

At last the morning came without a sunrise. A blizzard deals in paradoxes. It was not day: it was as if an evil spirit had travestied God's sunlight!

The storm grew stronger. A blizzard has the impetuosity of youth upon the first day, the strength of manhood upon the second, and upon the third day it grows peevish with senility and dies in the evening. In the sense of time, it is little more than an ephemeron. To its victims it is thrice a centenarian!

When the mockery of the day came, the people took heart and began to reconstruct their places of shelter. Yet scarcely had they cooked and eaten their morning meal when an order to take the trail came from Wazhinga Saba. A part hesitated; a part, whose fear of the chief was greater than the fear of the elements, prepared for the march; the remainder followed.

The long file disappeared into the swirling haze. It is true that the Chief also suffered; yet his selfishness was so great that to reach its ends, it ignored self. It was the apotheosis of egotism. Selfishness can become an inexorable god.

The hundreds of stumbling hoofs and feet left no

trail. A foot-print was momentary and served only to catch the drifting snow. Many wandered from the column into the terrible loneliness of the storm and never re-appeared. Many more tottered with weakness and the cold and lay where they fell. Those who followed stumbled across these unfortunates, and felt no pity. Despair crept icily through the blood of the tribe.

Despair is pitiless because it is the annihilation of all passion and the exaltation of egotism. It is that condition of the mind when the democratic government of the passions is cast down and the ego seizes the throne of reason, becoming dictatorial in defense of its realm.

The tribe was desperate. There is a terrible strength and power of endurance in desperation. Hope avails to goad the limbs only until that moment when the limbs become feeble; then it vanishes in terror and despair fights defeat. More heroes have been made by the probability of failure than by the possibility of success. It is the difference between the narcotic and the stimulant.

With his teeth set and his face to the east, Wazadi led his people into the storm. Even he had forgotten the meaning of pity. There was rage in his heart; the rage of a brave man who is a fighter and takes great odds. The coward grows tender in the midst of danger. The brave man grows angry.

Wazadi struck at the storm with his clenched fists! He wished that the wind would materialize into a bear that he might grapple with it and die with his teeth set in its neck.

But a storm is an anger without intelligence; a bodiless

foe; an enemy without nerves! It knows not its strength of offense and feels no blow of defense. It is irresistible and invulnerable.

The day lingered like a century, and when it had passed it was like a dream. The nights were terrible. Inaction lessens courage and increases suffering. Thus the three days passed, and the wind died. The white prairie emerged from the terrible shadow and the sun went down smiling like a cynic.

Wazadi looked upon his people and his heart grew sick. Hundreds were missing, and the survivors were shadows of men. Many of the ponies had strayed into the storm, dragging with them the children, the sick and the old. And a great wail shook the frozen air. It was the return of conscious suffering after delirium.

But upon the next morning the tribe again took up the trail, and when the sun of the twelfth day reached the highest point in its brief arc, a great shout went up from the foremost of the tribe, for the broad, frozen river lay before them, and the trail was ended.

Immediately the entire tribe began the difficult task of building lodges from the frozen ground. The young and old, the squaws and the braves, threw their feeble efforts into the work and their hearts grew warm again with the warmth that clings about a home. They felt no hatred against their chief for their past suffering; no more than the sleeper feels against the night when awakened from a nightmare. They had not forgiven; they had forgotten. Joy was gigantic and left no nook for the dwelling place of hate.

In a few days the village was complete, and the tribe again settled down for the winter. But Wazhinga Saba was not happy. His heart was dull with the tedium that follows a dead triumph. The Chief wanted diversion; he wanted feasting merriment. Therefore he sent runners about the village collecting a certain amount of meat from each lodge; and the people groaned as they gave, for they could see starvation stalking through the months of spring.

Then, for many months Wazhinga Saba ate with his puppet chiefs; and there was much laughter in the big lodge, much groaning without.

But the feasting lost its flavor and Wazhinga Saba longed for new pleasures. He found no beauty in his old women; years and toil and suffering had seamed their faces. Again he sent runners about the village, and this time they demanded the fairest of the maidens, whom he smiled upon in the evening and frowned upon in the morning.

To a primitive Indian, women were inviolate. They might toil and suffer, but they dared not be impure. An impure woman would have been stoned from the village.

So a great murmur of anger grew among the lodges; and all this indefinite muttering rage gathered and centralized in one voice. That voice was Wazadi. He stood in the center of a growing crowd of his tribesmen, and his voice was loud and fearless:

"Does my cry reach the ears of badgers? Are you brave but deaf? Are you strong but blind? Did Wakunda make the prairie and the people for Wazhinga Saba? Was it not enough that he gave us to be bitten by the winds? Are we wolves that we turn and flee not? The love which I gave to you at the summer's end, that love continues. I made you well; but Wazhinga Saba is worse sickness. Let us put this sickness from us!"

When the fearless youth had ceased speaking he became the center of a great shouting.

"Lead us! Be our chief!" the people cried.

"Wazadi will be your brother," he answered, "your brother and your chief. Let us build a village of our own where Wazhinga Saba will not be."

The last words went among the people and divided them. Many shouted with approval; many only scowled and shook their heads. Their fear was greater than their hate.

That day Wazadi led his party carrying all its baggage out of the old village into the hills to the north, and there a new village was built. And the people of his party changed the bold youth's name, calling him Tawagaha (little village maker), and the name clung, and to this day it is as a great noise in the ears of the Omahas.

The winter grew old; the sun crept northward; the southwinds blew. The great hoarse voice of the river with its booming ice went like a herald before the approach of spring. The snow faded from the hills. The meadow-larks and the kildeers came back; the gophers chattered. The days grew balmy and the frogs sang again. The last ice of the winter crashed past and the big muddy river exulted like a thing with a heart. Greenness and warmth and sweet scents!

In either village there was not a throat that could not sing, save one. Wazhinga Saba still held the winter at his heart. The shadow of his hate preserved the snow of his soul. While the broad sky and the vast prairie relented, he thought only of revenge.

Nothing can invent like a hate that lingers. It is a diabolical genius. It would burn away where love would wilt and weep. This is because it has nothing to lose; it has all to gain. If Leander had taken the flood that he might kill a sleeping rival, the Hellespont would have been narrower.

Wazhinga Saba sat in his lodge and plotted. He knew that the people believed him to be a terrible medicine man, a doer of magic things; yet he knew all his past successes to have depended merely upon trickery. Therefore he would not depend upon magic for his revenge, but merely as an appropriate setting for that revenge.

Several years before, the steamboats of the white man had sailed up the Missouri as far as the place where the Omahas were now camped, the American Fur Company having established a trading post in 1810 at Bellevue at a distance of about 150 miles down stream.

Every spring and fall since then the company's boat, St. Ange, had made a trip to the foot of Blackbird Hill, where the Omahas had their winter village, in order to trade for the valuable furs which the Indians disposed of very cheaply.

Ever since Columbus first trod the American shore, the Indian has looked upon the white man as a being of superior powers; and the Omaha was no exception. Did not the Wahgah (big knife or white man) know the magic that made the talking stick and the sticks that walk? Did he not chain fire in the belly of his big canoe and make it snort with toil? Then might he not also possess some great mysterious medicine?

Sometimes thus ran the thoughts of Wazhinga Saba, and his heart became glad with the gladness of a young revenge. He had at last formed a great plan.

One evening during the time when the squaws pull the weeds in the gardens (May), runners, sent to watch the river from the bluffs, came puffing into the tepee of Wazhinga Saba. "Monda Tonga! (big canoe) Wahgah! Wahgah!" they cried, motioning excitedly toward the river. At that moment the long sonorous howl of a steamboat's whistle came from the south and echoed in the bluffs. The Chief leaped to his feet, his face glowing with a great joy.

"Go! Bring the Wahgah to Wazhinga Saba!" he cried, and the runners bounded out of the tepee and disappeared in the direction of the river. An hour later a half dozen white men led by the runners and followed by a curious mob of Omahas, approached the tepee of the Great Chief. The rabble, however, satisfied its curiosity at a respectful distance from the "talking sticks" which the traders carried.

With much ceremony Wazhinga Saba received his white brothers, and dispersed the crowd with a motion of his arm. The traders, through their interpreter, at once set about displaying a stock of gaudy trifles, but Wazhinga Saba would have none of them. He forthwith explained his peculiar needs.

"He wants some kind of strong medicine," said the interpreter to the traders.

"Tell him about whiskey," they said.

The interpreter talked with the Chief in the Omaha tongue.

"He wants to know what it can do," said the interpreter laughing.

"Make much crazy," volunteered the traders, executing an extravagant pantomime of drunkenness: "So!"

Wazhinga Saba's face beamed as he watched the white man's insane evolutions. Perhaps he was mentally putting Tawagaha in the same ridiculous position. Yes! that was the medicine he wanted!

The interpreter explained, with much recourse to hyperbole, the great value of the medicine in question, and the Chief answered by showing the big stack of bison hides which he would give for ever so little. When a rich child wants anything a trade is easy; and when the traders withdrew from the Chief's tepee, Wazhinga Saba sat gloating over a jug of "medicine."

The next morning the St. Ange, well-stocked with buffalo hides, took the current, whistling like a live thing glad of a full stomach, and the Omahas took up their usual routine of life.

One morning a runner left the tepee of Wazhinga Saba and took his way to Tawagaha's village. He entered the tepee of the self-constituted chief and spoke kind things into his ear for Wazhinga Saba. It was represented with many honeyed words that the Big Chief's heart ached with his past unkindness to Tawagaha, with whom he wished to talk and feast that the past might be as a dead thing.

Tawagaha, having the tender heart which goes with generosity, at once arose and followed the runner to the tepee of Wazhinga Saba, where many other sweet words met his ear.

They feasted and smoked the peace pipe, and Tawagaha forgot. At last Wazhinga Saba produced an earthen bowl containing a copper-colored liquid.

"Wazhinga Saba has talked much with the good spirits," said the Big Chief. "Here is the water of kindness: drink and we shall be friends."

Tawagaha looked suspiciously at the mysterious water.

"See!" said Wazhinga Saba, "it is colored with the color of the evening after a day of winds. Wazhinga Saba has been cruel like the winds, and this is the evening of his hate. Drink, and there shall be a big sunrise of friendship!"

Tawagaha raised the earthen bowl to his lips.

"It is the gift of the good spirits," said the Big Chief, coaxingly.

Tawagaha drank great draughts, and set the bowl down.

"It bites!" he said.

"Like hate!" said Wazhinga Saba.

After a silence Tawagaha frowned.

"It gnaws!" said he.

"Like cruel words," said the Chief.

Tawagaha sat for some time like one stunned. Then he grasped his head with both hands and leaped to his feet.

"It tickles!" he shrieked, and leaped out of the tepee yelling and beating his head with his fists. He dashed through the village and the people scattered before him. Civilization had not yet given them a broad understanding!

Tawagaha shouted and laughed and shrieked. He danced and struck enormous blows at an imaginary enemy, and ran howling to his village. When he had disappeared, Wazhinga Saba came out of his tepee and spoke grave words to his startled people.

"Tawagaha's head is on fire," he said. "Wakunda has punished him for his deed against the great Wazhinga Saba! Let none follow Tawagaha!"

The people trembled as they heard. They shook their heads and were glad that they had not followed the daring youth. The same day a crier went through the village of Tawagaha and repeated the words of the Chief in a loud voice:

"Come back to the village of Wazhinga Saba," he cried; "the Great Chief loves his people and would protect them from evil spirits."

A primitive Indian was always superstitious first and generous afterward. He would do more for the fear of a black spirit than for the love of a leader. So it happened that the people of the little village at once moved to the larger village, again coming under the control of Wa-zhinga Saba.

Then spring came to the heart of the Chief, and he could smile again.

But Tawagaha, having fallen into a heavy slumber in his tepee, awoke the next day and the fire was dead in his brain. He arose and walked about his village, but found it deserted. He stopped and thought deeply, as if trying to recollect a vague dream. At last he remembered the mysterious liquid. Then all was clear to him. He knew whither his people had gone, and he walked toward the larger village with a heavy heart.

When he entered the village there was none to give him greeting. His own people looked at him trem-blingly, and fled from him. He wandered through the village, but everywhere it was the same. It was like a ghost roaming through a village of ghosts. None spoke to him. Everywhere the people shook their heads and shut themselves in their tepees. The very children hid at his coming and peered after him when he had passed.

Then Tawagaha gave a great cry of despair that was followed only by the silence. When the people ventured to come out of their tepees, Tawagaha had disappeared.

The summer came—a burning summer. The prairie is a double wonder. It can blossom like an oasis and burn like a Sahara. The breath of the winds is its life or its death. The Southwest strikes it barren.

In the beginning of the month of the bellowing of the bulls (July), the terrible wind awakened. The prairie grew sallow as the skin of an impoverished thing. The corn in the gardens wilted. The creeks were anaemic veins creeping sluggishly into the river that dwindled to a creek. The great smoky water was as a giant stricken with fever. Its sandbars were as the protrusions of mighty ribs.

The people sent up a wail like the echo of the Southwest's moan. And there was much crying after the rain, but no cloud reared its white head from under the dazzling horizon.

Wazhinga Saba sang a thunder song, but the rain spirits were deaf. The blue basins of the rain were dried up.

But one evening as the people sat about their tepees talking about the rains that did not come, the sound of a wild voice arose upon the dull air. The people sat charmed into breathlessness and listened. They recognized the mysterious syllables of the thunder song. Who was the singer? Was it a spirit?

In answer to the silent question the naked form of a man, emaciated as with famine, walked with slow steps through the village. His head was thrown back and his lips were parted with ecstatic song.

As the people looked upon the face of the singer they shuddered, for it was the face of Tawagaha! He passed on through the village chanting the song that the thunder spirits love, and disappeared.

That night it happened that the clouds gathered and thundered and the rain came in torrents. When the day dawned, the people's voices gathered into a great cry:

"It was Tawagaha! He brought the rain! Where is Tawagaha?" The shout echoed in the steaming hills and the hills sent back an answer. The answer was a man who walked with the swift step of happy feet toward the village.

Thus was Tawagaha re-instated in the people's favor. And Wazhinga Saba's hate grew like a wilted thing that has been watered with the rains.

The summer passed and the fall came, and with it came the trading boat, St. Ange. Again the traders were conducted to the lodge of the Big Chief. One of the white men, with a broad grin upon his face, asked through the interpreter if the medicine of last spring had acted properly.

"Ninga! Peazha!" replied the Chief, shaking his head decidedly.

"He says it was no good!" explained the interpreter.

"Ask him what he wants now?" said one of the white men.

The interpreter spoke briefly to the Chief, who began to explain with much impersonation of description, contorting his face, writhing with his body and at last falling in a tragic representation of death.

"He wants something that will hurt much and kill," the interpreter explained.

"Strychnine!" suggested one of the traders.

"Think we've got some on the boat," added another; and a man was forthwith sent after the desired medicine. He soon returned and displayed a small phial containing a white granular substance.

"This will kill," said the interpreter to the Chief.

Wazhinga Saba became excited. He offered a stack of

buffalo hides as high as his knees. The traders shook their heads. Then the chief doubled the imaginary pile. Still there was no trade.

"What will it do? Show me," said the Chief to the interpreter. A dog had followed one of the white men and now it ran about expressing good humor with its sinuous tail. A piece of meat was procured from the Chief and a small particle of strychnine placed upon it. This was fed to the dog, who ate it greedily. Suddenly its eyes became glazed; it fell howling to the ground, writhed, and died!

The Chief's eyes blazed. He pointed to the peak of the tepee and swung his arm about him, thus saying that he would fill his tepee with buffalo hides in exchange for the medicine.

The trade was made, and when the hides had been collected from among the people of the village, the white men withdrew groaning beneath their spoils.

Forthwith the wily Wazhinga Saba set his brain in motion; it had become a diabolical machine propelled by hate. He knew that Tawagaha would refuse to feast with him again; so he decided to feast with Tawagaha. He waited four days (for four is a magic number) and upon the fourth evening he went, humbly dressed, to the tepee of his rival. He entered and fell upon his face before the youth, groaning as with great mental anguish.

The heart of Tawagaha, like all great hearts, was pitiful. He raised the Chief and told him to speak his grief.

"The days of Wazhinga Saba have been many," began the Chief, sniveling with a burlesque grief, "many and cruel. Now his head is white and his strength passes. Does the young man feel no pity for the old? We have been enemies, but Wazhinga Saba has become as a snake without fangs. Pity him, and you shall be his chief!"

Tawagaha heard and was deceived.

"Tawagaha pities," said he; "let us smoke the peace pipe and eat together that we may be friends."

The two smoked. Then Tawagaha's squaw placed an iron kettle, bought from the white men, over a fire, and boiled a great piece of buffalo meat.

When the meat was cooked, Wazhinga Saba arose and bowing over the kettle, dropped something into it. "The blessing of an old man is good," he said.

Tawagaha opened the feast, bulging his cheeks with a liberal bite. The old man watched.

Suddenly the face of the young man grew livid. He shrieked and fell to the floor, writhing and groaning in terrible agony. His strong limbs contracted; his muscles stood out in knots; his veins swelled blue. Then with a last great effort he muttered a curse upon his smiling enemy, and died.

Wazhinga Saba heard the curse and his triumph brought him terror. He fled to his tepee and shut himself up for many days.

There was much wonder among the people, and when the boldest ventured to question the old chief concerning the death of Tawagaha he could only groan.

Some years after Wazhinga Saba fell ill with the small-pox, and believing it to be the curse of Tawagaha, he died in terror.

I have stood upon a high hill of the present Omaha Reservation. It is known as the Blackbird Hill, for there the terrible chief was buried, sitting upon his horse with all his arms about him, that he might see the Big Knives (white men) come up the river in their fire-breathing canoes, as he said.

As I stood there I felt both admiration and pity. But when I asked an old Omaha about the dread chief, he scowled and would not answer. The memory of wrongs lives long and dies slowly.

Overland Monthly, July 1903

The End of the Dream

The old woman Gunthai had nothing but a past over which she brooded and a son upon whom she doted. Had she been able to write the latter in the letters of that tongue which came to the prairie many moons after her death, breaking with syllables of magic the spell of the centuries, she would have written it with a "u"; for her son was as the day to her; his coming was the morning and his going was the sunset. When he laughed, there was summer in the wretched little tepee; when he cried, the snows drifted about the mother-heart.

Winter and summer the old woman sat in her lodge, her back bent with the burdens of many seasons and her face seamed with many memories; yet stern and expressionless as of one who has followed a long trail and cannot see its end though the sun be falling.

All day she would sit in her lodge, weaving baskets of willow, which she exchanged with her tribesmen for meat and robes; for the father of her child was dead. Her little boy, whom she tenderly called Nu Zhinga (Little Man), would lie long hours before her with his chin resting upon his little brown hands, watching the fingers

100

of his mother weave the pliant twigs into form with marvellous skill, as it seemed to him; and often when the hours crept lamely, he would sing to her a monotonous song like the wind's, timing the irregular air with the beating of his toes upon the floor.

And when the little singer would cease, the old woman Gunthai often forgot the unwoven basket with gazing into his big black eyes, for in them her hope could read great deeds that were to be done after many unborn moons had waned.

Then she would tell him tales of his father; tales that were loud with the snarl of war drums, the twang of bow thongs, the shriek of arrows, the beat of hoofs! But there was no responsive glitter in the eyes of the boy; his heart was not the warrior's, and the old mother seeing this, sighed and fell to work with nervous haste.

And the days of sun and snow wove themselves into years, until Nu Zhinga had reached that time when boyhood begins to deepen into manhood; and yet as the mother looked upon her son, she found him scarcely taller than a weak man's bow.

His legs were short and bowed, his hips narrow, and upon shoulders of abnormal breadth sat his monstrous, shaggy head. It was as if he were the visible body of a black spirit's joke, save for his lustrous eyes, that were like two stars that burn big in the air of evening through a film of mist.

And thus it was that when Nu Zhinga passed through the village, those who were still foolish with youth jeered at the lad, calling his name in contempt; but the old men and women who had grown wise, only shook their heads and pitied Gunthai in silence.

But the boy would take no notice of his tormentors, walking on sullen and silent. He lived in a little world of his own, which was isolated from the great world by the unkindness of his people, like a range of frozen hills; and in this small world there were but three dwellers: Gunthai, a tame grey wolf, and one other. That other was a despised little cripple and her name was Tabea (Frog).

These three, and about them the chromatic glory of dreams like a sunrise that lingers—this was the world of Nu Zhinga. All day amid the quiet of the summer hills Nu Zhinga and Tabea played together; he telling of the great indefinite things that he would do in that big mysterious sometime when the days would be pregnant with wonders! For in his soul the pulse of uncertain but lofty resolve bounded, and as he peered into the future, lo! it was vast, yet dim with misty possibilities like a broad stretch of prairie expanding under the new moon! And she, with all of her crooked little body attentive, listened and believed even more than she heard; which is the way of those who love.

And then these two, after the manner of children, would play at life, building a tepee with willows from a convenient creek; and Tabea would groan as she bore the heavy burdens, thus showing how she would toil for him and suffer. Then when the tepee was built, she would go about droning a song, with her back bent as with the weight of an infant, thus showing how she

would carry the child of Nu Zhinga in that big and sunlit
sometime.

One day when the last white footstep of the winter
had vanished from the coldest valley, the old woman
Gunthai laid aside a finished basket and called her boy to
her side.

"It is the time," she said; "the time is ripe with summers. Nu Zhinga must eat no meat for four days; then he
must go to the hill where the visions come, that he may
know what is to be for him in the light of the unborn
moons."

So Nu Zhinga ate no meat for four days, and when the
fourth evening came, as the fires roared upward among
the circled lodges, he passed through the village and took
his way to the high hill of dreams. It was the time when
the valleys are loud with the song of frogs and when the
Earth begins to learn anew the pleasant lesson of the Sun.

When he had stopped, breathless with toiling up the
long incline, for he was weak with hunger, he turned and
looked back upon the jumbled village and saw, indis-
tinctly through the mist of the evening, his mother
standing before the door of her lodge, straining her gaze
that she might see her boy for the last time, climbing to
the height where the dream awaited, that should send
him back a man with a future big in deeds.

Then Nu Zhinga climbed on to the summit of the hill
and watched the west pass from brilliant colours into
dun, and the darkness come with the stars. In the light of
a thin moon the far hills whitened. The big stars glowed

THE END OF THE DREAM

kindly like the camp fires of a friendly people. The night
wind talked to itself in the gulches; and attentive to these,
Nu Zhinga forgot the reason of his coming, and lulled
by the many pleasant sounds, fell asleep and was awakened by the pale damp Dawn.

Then he ran down the hill, and as he passed through
the village, the old women, some busy about the steaming kettles, others bent beneath the loads of fuel, shook
their heads and said: "Gunthai's boy has had no vision;
not so do they return who dream great dreams."

In the doorway of her lodge Gunthai stood awaiting
the approach of her son. Her body that was wont to be
bent like a bow upon which a heavy hand is laid in anger,
was erect and quivering as is the bow when the arrow has
sped like a purpose. Upon her leathery, wrinkled face
dwelt the glimmer of an inner illumination. Only the
flesh was old, the light was young; for Hope is a youth.

As the lad approached, the tenseness of expectation
held the old woman's tongue and her question came
from her eyes. "What has Nu Zhinga dreamed?"

"I saw the stars that were like the eyes of a friend,"
said the boy, "and I heard the wind as it sang to itself in
the gulches. I slept and awoke, and lo! the sun was
teaching gladness to the hills!"

Many seasons sit lightly upon a form when Hope sits
with them; but Despair is heavy, and again the weight of
many years bent the shoulders of the mother. When the
sun leaves a cloud of glory, it leaves a mass of murk; thus
passed the light from the wrinkled face of Gunthai.

There was a sigh in her voice as she spoke; a sigh like

104

that of a wind that is heavy with rain: "There should have come a dream loud with the noises of battle and shrill with the flight of arrows! Thus did your father dream."

So Nu Zhinga went a second and a third and a fourth time to the hill of dreams, and the last answer that his mother heard was like the first. And on the fifth day the heart of the old mother was sore with sorrow, and all that night she did not sleep, but wept and moaned: "How shall Gunthai be comforted when her eyes are dim and her fingers stiff? Her son shall not be mighty in the hunt and battle, for he has had no dream."

The lad, awakened in the night by the moaning of his mother, knew in an indefinite way that he was the cause of so much grief; and in his breast grew a great pang of soul hunger that would not pass away. Even with the giant joy of the sunrise it did not pass away.

In the early light Nu Zhinga passed out of the village, for his heart was heavy. As he walked, lo! everything was sad except the sun, and the light of its gladness deepened the shadow of his sorrow. The sound of the wind moving in the bunch grass of the hillside was like a faint cry of a great pain. At length he threw himself down and buried his face in the grass. The despair of those who dream daydreams was upon him. There was night in his heart; his small body shook with sobs. A long while he lay thus, nor did he hear the soft step that stopped beside him.

At length Nu Zhinga raised his head from the grass and saw Tabea sitting beside him with pity in her eyes and in the attitude of her crooked little body. Without a word they stared each into the face of the other; and as Nu Zhinga looked, the desolate grey of the world began to develop its wonted brilliance of colour, as though the union of their tears had produced a prism.

At length these two arose and walked among the hills, dreaming as was their wont, and again the sunlight entered the heart of Nu Zhinga. When the two outcasts entered the village, even though the youths trooped behind them shouting "Peazha!" (no good), yet the sunlight did not pass; for upon one hand walked the dreams of Nu Zhinga and upon the other, Tabea.

One day in the time of the gathering of the maize, when the brown hills shivered with the first frosts, the voice of a crier was heard through the village calling the braves to battle; for the big chief of the Omahas would lead a war party against the Sioux.

So the old woman Gunthai took down the weapons of her fallen brave from the side of the tepee where they had hung in idleness for many moons. She strung the long unbent bow with a thong of buckskin and retipped the arrows with the feathers of the hawk. Then she wept over them, and blessed them with weird songs; and calling Nu Zhinga to her side, placed them in his hands, and said: "Bring them back red with the blood of the Sioux!"

And the youth took them, wondering why it was so very great a thing to kill.

Then the war party rode out of the village and Nu Zhinga rode with it. And there were two who climbed to the highest hill and, shading their eyes with their hands, watched the braves disappear into the distance. They were Gunthai and Tabea, and the hopes of each were great. For might not even Nu Zhinga do great deeds? Such things had been.

After many days the returning band rode up the valley that rang with the song of victory. But when it rode into the village, a great cry went up against Nu Zhinga, the squaw-hearted. For in the battle with the Sioux his pony had fallen with an arrow in its breast, and when the Omahas returned from the pitiless pursuit of their flying foes, they found him crying like a squaw over the carcass of the animal.

When the people heard this concerning Nu Zhinga, an angry cry, like that of a strong wind in a thicket, passed over the multitude gathered about the braves. "Let him go work with the squaws!" they cried. And the unanimous cry of a people is a law.

So Nu Zhinga, the squaw-hearted, carried water and wood with the women and was patient. At least he had Tabea ever near him, which was like living in the light of perpetual sunrise, and hope, like an incurable disease, would not leave his breast.

The old woman Gunthai seeing how more than squaw-hearted her son had grown, sat in her lodge weaving the baskets of willow. But the hope of her heart was gone. How she had dreamed of the prowess of her little man! How he would be mighty among his people; mighty with the arm that is pitiless and strong—a slayer of enemies! But now—and the old woman's thought would check itself at that barren gulch in the hills through which Death comes like a blast of bitter winds, for she could see no further.

So the suns came and went; but there was night for her in the brightest noon; the seasons passed, but for her heart there was cold, even in the kind midsummer.

One day in the time of the cubs (December) it happened that a child of the village was stricken with a mysterious sickness. The fierce heat of the time of the sunflowers blazed in its blood. Its eyes glowed with the brightness of a burning thing. Its lips muttered strange words that were not the words of men; and those who listened, trembled. And after some time, the whole burning body of the child became one mass of sores.

It was then that Washkahee, the big medicine-man, came to the lodge of the sick, sang his most potent songs and performed his most mysterious rites. But one day the child leaped to its feet and stared at the wall with eyes that were glazed with terror; then shrieked and fell back limply into its blankets. And when the winter had crept into its burning blood, they buried it upon a hill; and the wonder of the village was great.

But the end was not yet. Another and another crept into his blankets, stricken with the same sickness. Then another and another, until from many lodges came the moans of the afflicted. Those who dwelt in the lodges where the scourge entered, fled from their stricken kinsmen as from the visible body of Death. They who could laugh back at the challenge of the Sioux, quailed before the subtle creeping of this invisible foe. They who were as yet untouched by the unseen Hand, huddled terrified and speechless about their fires, in the light of which they stared at each other and found each face ghastly, as though it were the mirror of their dread.

In the stillness of their bated breaths they heard the lonesome monotony of the winter wind and the swish of the drifting snow, through the drone of which pierced like arrows of ice the occasional shrieks of the deserted dying or those who battled with grotesque terrors in the giddy whirl of feverish delirium.

With trembling fingers the women bound blankets closely across the doors of the lodges, in the hope of barring out the black spirit that wandered about the village. Vain hope! Through the walls of the strongest lodge crept the subtle spirit.

One night the sound of a wild voice crying through the storm beat into the lodges:

"Washkahee has cried to Wakunda [God] and lo! Washkahee has dreamed! Only a tuft of hair from the head of the white bison can save us! So spoke the dream to Washkahee; who will seek the white bison?"

It was as though the winter wind had found words! The people, huddled about their fires, knew the voice to be that of the big medicine-man, Washkahee, yet they did not move. The bravest had become weak as a child at the back of a squaw.

That night Nu Zhinga, lying in the lodge of his mother, heard the cry that came out of the storm; and when he slept he dreamed. He had walked far across the white prairie and his legs were aching with toil and his heart with despair. Then there broke upon his dream a mighty roar, and lo! he saw, charging down upon him, the white bison, tossing the crusted snow from its lowered horns.

"Tae Ska! Tae Ska!" (white bison) Nu Zhinga cried, and was awakened by his own voice.

So in the early light of the morning, Nu Zhinga took down the bow and arrows of his father, and wrapping himself in a buffalo robe, he strode out into the prairie with his tame wolf trotting at his heels. To him the dream was an omen. Might he not find the white bison, and thus drive death from among his people?

As he walked, the dream that had ever crept like a slow music through his blood, grew into the swaying fury of a battle-song. He timed his brisk steps with a joyous chant that echoed up the frosty valleys. He would find the white bison! Then his people would shout his name without derision. Gunthai would be glad; Tabea would be glad. Tabea! The word was music.

But meanwhile in the village thicker and thicker fell the invisible arrows of the Terror; and in the lodges where they fell dwelt the cry of agony and delirium and the muffled shriek of death. The old woman Gunthai and the cripple Tabea were not spared. The old and the young, the weak and the strong, the brave and the cowardly found no spell to ward away the stroke of the hidden Hand.

At length the fear of the tribe grew into a frenzy. It needed but an incident to lash it into madness.

One evening as the night crept westward across the hills, a brave leaped upon a pony and yelling sent the frightened animal flying up the valley. He was fleeing from the curse that hung over the village. Then the fear became a madness. The people rushed from their lodges and, fighting for the nearest pony, fled after the lone rider who had disappeared into the night.

Those who were too weak or too unfortunate to gain the back of a pony hung to the mane and were dragged in the snow until their grips weakened, when they ran with frantic shrieks after their disappearing tribesmen. The valley leading from the village became choked with the fleeing people. Many of the stricken leaped from their blankets and followed in the wild rout, until their knees weakened and their brains swam, when they lay shriek-ing in the snow until death came.

From the deserted village the cries of the helpless followed the unhearing refugees, who fled as the bison flee when the pitiless hunter follows. Fainter and fainter grew the yelling until it was swallowed up in the wind that lashed the spraying snow. When the morning looked into the valley, it found no smoke arising from the silent lodges. Only the dead were there; the dead and the win-ter.

On the evening of the second day after the flight of the tribe, a lone form topped the hill above the village and looked down into the still white valley, where lay the snow-choked lodges, quiet as a dream. The form was short, and bent as with the toil and hunger of a long, hard trail. At its heels a gaunt, grey wolf limped and whim-pered with the ache of emptiness and the frost.

The short, bent form stood still upon the summit and

shading its eyes with a hand that trembled, cast a long and searching gaze upon the lodges of his people. No smoke, no voice, no roar of fires, scented with the evening meal!

The form straightened itself and stood with head thrown back, making a thin and pitiful figure against the cruel white glare of the icy evening sky. It put a hand to its mouth, trumpet-wise, and raising the other above its head, waved about a tuft of long, grey hair.

"Tae Ska! Tae Ska!"

The voice was scarcely raised above a faint, dry wheeze that sighed dirge-like above the lifeless valley. The grey wolf with its four trembling legs drawn together in the snow, raised its frost-whitened muzzle to the fading sky and with a long, wild wail drowned the feebler voice of its master.

With limping stride, grown short and uncertain as the first steps of a papoose, the form went down the hillside and entered the village where the Winter dwelt.

"Tae Ska! Tae Ska! I have found the white bison!"

The wheezing voice passed among the lodges like a mournful wind that haunts the lonesome places of a bluff. Round and round the village went the man and the wolf, crying into the silent lodges; and the man's face was wolflike with weariness and hunger; and the wolf's eyes were grown half human with the pinch of emptiness and frost.

"Why do you not come forth, for I have suffered and I have the tuft of hair? No more shall the black spirits dwell among us! Come forth and look upon the face of him whose heart was the heart of a squaw!"

The crisp snow whined beneath his step and the wolf whined beside him. At last the form stopped before a lodge and with a trembling hand drew away the covering at the entrance.

It was the lodge of Gunthai. Two forms lay within, huddled in their blankets, and the snows had drifted about them. The man pulled the blankets from their faces. One was Gunthai and the other Tabea. Each was pinched with the pinch of death and winter, and the mystery of the last long, lonesome trail was about them both.

With a moan the form tottered and fell upon its face in the snow. And over all the valley there were but two sounds—the wail of the winter wind and the howl of a lone wolf.

Days passed, and the people who had fled from home with the pitiless scourge at their heels grew faint and weary with their wandering, and at last the homeache drove them back upon their trail. Footsore, famished, racked with the now dread terror, they toiled in silence homeward, where they could die with the sound of their own fires in their ears.

At last one morning a lone rider cautiously peered from under the brow of the hill upon the village. Nothing moved below. He urged his emaciated pony to the summit of the hill and stopping, gazed again, shading his eyes with a hand grown weak and thin. There seemed nothing in the valley to fear. Turning about upon his pony, he raised his arms in the light of dawn and cried back into the valley beyond to the waiting remnant of his people—a long, exultant cry, for he had looked upon his home.

Slowly the returning tribe, now dwindled to half its former numbers, toiled up the hill. Only the strong were left, and now the strong were weak. The straggling band of men, women and ponies reached the summit, a pitiful, ragged multitude, and gazed for a moment into the valley. Then a great shout arose above the silent spaces, scintillant under the dawn, as the halting, famished band swooped down the hill to be again at home.

Again the fires roared upward from the lodges, and the voices of a happy people drove away the silence of the winter. There was no longer any disease; the winter and the flight had purged the tribe.

Who had saved them from the black spirits? Could a tribe run faster than the things which are not good?

The sun was at the center of its short path when the answer to this question of the tribe broke into the lodges where the people sat about their steaming kettles. For it was then that one ran through the village waving a tuft of long, grey hair and startling the ears of his people with a shout:

"See! The tuft of hair from the head of the white bison! It has saved us; for do you not remember the words of Washkahee?"

The people rushed from their lodges and thronged about the man who held the tuft of hair.

"Who has found the white bison?" they cried.

And the answer of him who held the tuft of hair struck the people silent with wonder:

"It was Nu Zhinga, the squaw-hearted; even he who could not dream a dream!"

Overland Monthly, September 1905